COLLINS

HOW TO IDENTIFY

EDIBLE
MUSHROOMS

HarperCollins*Publishers*
77–85 Fulham Palace Road
London W6 8JB

02 01

6 8 10 9 7 5

First published 1996

Patrick Harding and Tony Lyon dedicate this book to Jean, Maureen and their countless students. Gill Tomblin dedicates this book to Dr David Pegler for her introduction to fungi.

Patrick Harding taught plant ecology to undergraduates for seven years prior to 1978 when he moved to the University of Sheffield where he developed a large programme of adult courses in the natural sciences. His other titles include Collins Gem Photoguide *Mushrooms & Toadstools*, and the forthcoming *How to Identify Trees*.

Tony Lyon has been a lecturer since 1969 in the Department of Animal and Plant Sciences, University of Sheffield, where he teaches fungal biology to undergraduates. He is an active member of the British Mycological Society and was awarded their Benefactor's Medal in 1996 for his contribution to both the Society and mycology.

Artist Gill Tomblin trained at Bath Academy of Art and the Central School of Art in London. She has illustrated many books on natural history, gardening and children's fiction and non-fiction.

ISBN 0 00 219984 X

Illustration on p.35 by Sir John Tenniel from *Alice's Adventures in Wonderland* by Lewis Carroll, reproduced with permission of Macmillan Children's Books

Designed by Wilderness design, Rochester, Kent
Colour reproduction by Colourscan, Singapore
printed and bound by Rotolito Lombarda SpA, Milan, Italy

COLLINS

HOW TO IDENTIFY

EDIBLE
MUSHROOMS

PATRICK HARDING • TONY LYON • GILL TOMBLIN

HarperCollins*Publishers*

CONTENTS

Contents

Mushroom or Toadstool?

THE TWO WORDS ARE OFTEN USED INTERCHANGEABLY to mean any fleshy umbrella-shaped fungal fruitbody. However some people have tended to restrict 'mushroom' to edible species and 'toadstool' to poisonous ones. There seems to be little justification for such a distinction; the two words have long been synonymous but appear to have entered our language from different sources (Baker, 1989 and 1990; Morgan, 1987).

The English name toadstool, like the Scottish paddockstool and the Dutch paddestoel, suggests an association between toadstools and toads which is found in other languages such as French, Scandinavian, Ukrainian and Welsh. It has been used in this country at least since the 14th century. Its origins probably reflect common attitudes of revulsion towards both toads and toadstools which may at least in part derive from their suggested use by witches, but also reflects the contemporary view that they both arose from slimy origins.

This basic sliminess may also be behind the name 'mushroom'. This was probably derived from the old French 'moisseron', which itself most likely came from the Greek word 'μυκης', which also gave us the Latin word mucus and is the root of the term mycology, the name given to the scientific study of fungi.

We shall use both of these words as exact synonyms. A further complication arises because one group of fungi in the genus *Agaricus* is known as the Mushrooms, such as the Field Mushroom (see p. 47), and the Horse Mushroom (see p. 50), but, as we shall see, there are some poisonous Mushrooms and plenty of so-called toadstools that are good to eat.

Fig 1: Toad and toadstool

What are Mushrooms and Toadstools?

MUSHROOMS AND TOADSTOOLS ARE THE FRUITBODIES of particular types of fungi. At one time biologists used to consider all living organisms as members of either the plant or the animal kingdoms; fungi were thought of as plants which had lost their green pigment (chlorophyll). Now that we have a much greater understanding of the diversity of organisms, it is clear that species can be separated into at least five different kingdoms, one of which is devoted exclusively to the fungi. Although fungi share some of the features of both plants and animals, they differ in structure, ecology and biochemistry.

This view of fungi as organisms quite distinct from plants and animals is consistent with the way they are regarded by many traditional cultures (Morris 1988). There they are associated much more with the earth, either as 'a kind of excrement of the soil' as Francis Bacon put it, or as 'flor de tierra' (flowers of the earth), their name among the Purepecha of Mexico.

Many cultures classify fungi on the basis of their value as food. The Chewa of Malaya, for example, refer to edible mushrooms as 'nyama' or meat and this association with animal rather than plant life seems to be common. Interestingly, modern research shows that fungi do share several important chemical similarities with animals. Many fungi contain chitin, a substance commonly found in the external regions of insects.

Until recently Europeans have regarded fungi as lower plants and professional mycologists (those who study fungi) are mostly found in university Botany departments or attached to Botanic gardens such as Kew Gardens, London. Strictly speaking fungi should not be referred to as plants, but it is difficult to remember this when speaking of mushroom stems and fungal vegetative growth.

A fungus grows as a system of branching tubes, called hyphae, each hypha is approximately 0.01 mm in diameter. As the hyphae grow, the living material within (cytoplasm) tends to flow forwards into the newly formed tips, leaving the older parts of the hyphae with relatively little content. Eventually old hyphae may collapse and be degraded by other micro-organisms, particularly bacteria. Fungi have been described as 'animals that live in tubes' and it is possible to think of the cytoplasm as an organism that is constantly migrating, building new hyphal walls for protection as it moves.

The radiating system of branched hyphae, known as a mycelium, is almost entirely buried in the soil or within some organic material such as wood or leaf litter. As the outermost tips of the mycelium penetrate into previously unexplored territory, they are able to absorb nutrients which they use either to provide energy or to build up more of their own structure. Like animals, fungi are dependent on their surroundings for a supply of suitable food. All the fungi that we shall be considering in this book obtain this from either living or dead plant tissues, but there are some species for which animals (dead or alive) provide the food source while other fungi obtain their food from animal dung.

Fig 2: The germinating spore gives rise to a mycelium of branching hyphae.

Mycorrhizal fungi

Living plants contain a variety of sugars, amino-acids and minerals which are readily available to fungi. Hyphae are able to absorb these soluble nutrients directly and utilise them with the minimum of energy. However plants have evolved physical and chemical defences to prevent micro-organisms from exploiting their nutrients in this way, and those fungi that are able to do so have evolved ways of overcoming these defences.

One such group of fungi form an association with the roots of plants called a mycorrhiza (myco = fungus, rhiza = root). See Fig. 3a. Many of the woodland fungi described in this book are mycorrhizal with trees, e.g. all species of Bolete (*Boletus*), Milk Cap (*Lactarius*), *Russula* and *Amanita*. Many fungal species only form mycorrhizal associations with one, or very few, tree species, an important aid in the finding and identifying of particular species of mushroom.

The hyphae of such mycorrhizal fungi grow over the surface of the root, forming a dense fungal sheath. From this sheath, some hyphae grow in between the outer cells of the root, allowing transfer of nutrients between root and fungus. See Fig. 3b. Other hyphae grow out from the sheath into the soil where they are able to absorb mineral nutrients. The association between tree and mycorrhizal fungus is mutually beneficial; the fungus provides the tree with a supply of minerals whilst acquiring most of its sugars in return. Mycorrhizal associations tend to be most important in poor soils where the tree would find difficulty taking up minerals without the assistance of the fungus.

Decomposer fungi

As a plant dies, it is unable to maintain its defences against invasion by micro-organisms, so a much wider range of fungi is able to gain access to its nutrients. The declining plant fails to supply enough soluble sugars to satisfy a fungus so successful colonisers of dead plant tissue secrete enzymes that break down the structural chemicals of plant cell walls e.g. pectin, cellulose and lignin. The production of such enzymes is energy-demanding, but the fungus benefits by feeding on the breakdown products of their activity.

Different fungi tend to specialise in using particular plant tissues. For example Wood Blewit (*Lepista nuda*) and Stinking Puffball (*Lycoperdon foetidum*) grow in deciduous leaf litter, whereas Oyster Mushroom (*Pleurotus ostreatus*) and Velvet Shank (*Flammulina velutipes*) break down the wood of broad-leaved trees. Enzyme action weakens tissues, leads to physical disintegration and contributes to the process of decomposition.

Like most other organisms the majority of fungi are specialists – some species are found in grassland, others are associated with birch trees while some are only found in coniferous woods. On the

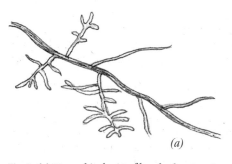

(a)

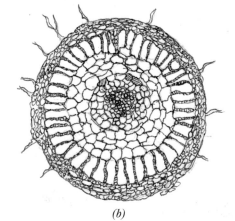

(b)

Fig. 3: (a) Mycorrhizal root of beech, showing short, stubby branches. (b) Cross-section of mycorrhizal root of beech, showing fungal sheath around the root (magnification x 20).

basis of this specialisation we have described the edible fungi under three habitat sections: Grassland, Broadleaved Woodland and Coniferous Woodland. No pigeon-holing in biology is foolproof; woods have grass on the rides and hedges provide homes for some woodland species, but a species restricted to rotting oak is unlikely to turn up in the middle of a lawn.

Fruiting

Fungi continue to grow and feed as long as there is an adequate supply of food and while environmental conditions remain favourable. It is very rare for both of these conditions to persist indefinitely. When growth becomes limited by stressful conditions such as food or water shortage or low temperature, most fungi respond by fruiting. In the case of mushrooms and toadstools, hyphae start to grow in little knots (called primordia) that develop into miniature fruitbodies. See Fig 4.

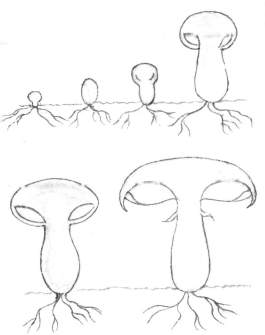

Fig. 4: Sequence of enlargement from primordium to mature fruitbody

The tiny fruitbodies may either remain at that stage of development or, under favourable conditions, grow very rapidly by taking up water from the mycelium. The final enlargement of nearby primordia is often suppressed by the presence of a mature fruitbody, just as the growth of side buds on a plant is suppressed by the main growing point. Picking a mushroom may then allow other primordia to mature.

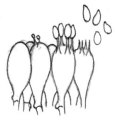

Fig. 5: Basidia with basidiospores

The fruitbody produces, and facilitates the dispersal of, spores. Spores perform the same function as seeds but lack a substantial food reserve. Edible fungi belong to two of the major divisions of the fungal kingdom, the ascomycetes and the basidiomycetes. Mushrooms and toadstools are fruitbodies of basidiomycete fungi. They have gills or pores whose surfaces are covered by a layer (called a hymenium) of cells (basidia) each of which bears four delicate points with a spore at the tip. (Fig. 5) At maturity the four spores are shot off from their basidium, fall under gravity until they are clear of the gills or pores and are then carried away by air currents. A few basidiomycetes do not discharge their spores in this way. For example the basidia of Puffballs mature within the fruitbody and lie inside until a hole develops through which they can escape.

A few edible fungi are ascomycetes; the Morels and Truffles being the most important. The fruitbody of an ascomycete fungus bears specialised cells (asci) which contain eight spores. (Fig. 6) At maturity, the asci squirt out their spores into the air, and they are blown away in the wind. In the Truffles the fruitbody develops underground; the asci do not release their spores. Instead the fruitbody emits an odour attracting animals searching

for food; they eat the Truffle and the spores are dispersed in their dung.

The majority of the spores remain inactive until certain favourable conditions stimulate germination. Further growth of the resulting hypha is dependent on the proximity of a suitable food source. Some fruitbodies produce many millions of spores, but very few of these will give rise to established individuals.

Longevity of fungi

Many mould fungi have a brief life-cycle. When the mycelium runs out of nutrients, virtually all the resources of the organism are put into spore production. However, the great majority of the fungi considered in this book have mycelia that may persist for many years. Only a part of the stored food reserves within the fungus are committed to fruiting, the remainder being used to sustain the mycelium. During periods when conditions are favourable the fungal colony continues to extend outwards, its progress being halted when conditions are too dry, cold, etc. As the cytoplasm is concentrated round the periphery of the mycelium, the colony acquires the form of a hollow ring, whose presence can be detected when it fruits, or by the appearance of a 'fairy ring' when growing in grassland (see p. 32).

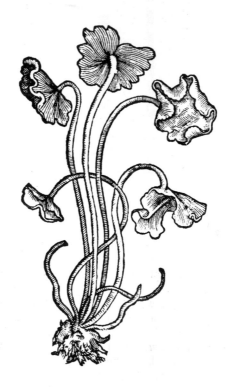

When do Fungi Fruit?

FOR MOST OF THE EDIBLE SPECIES DESCRIBED IN THIS BOOK we have included a histogram showing fruiting records in the North Midlands, based on 15 years of observation. The frequency of occurence in any month is proportional to the number of mushroom symbols. Some modification may need to be made for Cornwall or northern Scotland, but the histograms show that most edible species are not restricted to a single month. In a dry year a species may appear from September to December but given a wet summer it may fruit earlier; from June to September.

For too many people the search for edible fungi is restricted to the autumn, but it is possible to gather edible wild fungi of some sort at any season. In this book we have indicated that Cauliflower Fungus (*Sparassis crispa*) is an autumn species, but a fresh specimen was once found in early March.

A CALENDAR OF EDIBLE FUNGI

WINTER *(December to March)*

While the majority of fungal fruitbodies cannot withstand freezing temperatures there are a number of notable exceptions and four edible species are found throughout the winter:

Velvet Shank (*Flammulina velutipes* p. 136) which starts fruiting in the autumn but is much more obvious in the winter.

Oyster Mushroom (*Pleurotus ostreatus* p. 128) can be found all year but is more abundant in the winter months.

Wood Blewit (*Lepista nuda* p. 102) is really a late autumn species but continues to Christmas, and in mild winters can appear (especially in gardens) through to March.

Jew's Ear (*Auricularia auricula-judae* p. 146) occurs throughout the year but is more easily spotted during the winter, especially when growing on elder.

SPRING *(April and May)*

Two good edible species fruit only in the spring:

Morel (*Morchella esculenta* p. 122) and St. George's Mushroom (*Calocybe gambosa* p. 52). Late specimens can be found in June but the main flush is earlier.

Oyster Mushroom (*Pleurotus ostreatus* p. 128)

becomes less frequent and by late spring is largely replaced by Branched Oyster Mushroom (*Pleurotus cornucopiae* p. 130).

May is the peak time for finding one of the edible bracket fungi – Dryad's Saddle (*Polyporus squamosus* p. 143).

SUMMER *(June to August)*

June is a surprisingly good month for edible fungi as this is when the first mushrooms appear – Field Mushroom (*Agaricus campestris* p. 47) and Horse Mushroom (*Agaricus arvensis* p. 50)

together with Giant Puffball (*Langermania gigantea* p. 68) which is a typical summer species. Some autumn species start fruiting in June, especially in wet seasons, and include: Fairy Ring Champignon

(*Marasmius oreades* p. 66) and the edible Russulas (pp. 84–89), Boletes (pp. 92–99) and Puffballs (pp. 68–72). June is the peak month for fresh specimens of Sulphur Polypore (*Laetiporus sulphureus* p. 141) although it continues into autumn.

July is typically a poor fungus month especially in grassland (but look out for the Giant Puffball).

In contrast August can herald the start of the main flush for many woodland species such as Chanterelle (*Cantharellus cibarius* p. 114), Cep (*Boletus edulis* p. 92), Bay Bolete (*Xerocomus badius* p. 94), the two Birch Boletes (*Leccinum versipelle* and *Leccinum scabrum* pp. 96–99), Fawn Mushroom (*Pluteus cervinus* p. 132), the Deceiver (*Laccaria laccata* p. 112), Beefsteak Fungus (*Fistulina hepatica* p. 142) and Summer Truffle (*Tuber aestivum* p. 120).

AUTUMN *(September to November)*

September and October represent the high season both in terms of number of edible species and overall number of fruitbodies. In some years a wet summer brings a bumper September but following a long dry summer it may be well into October before conditions are ideal. Early frosts foreshorten the season but in mild years there are still many species fruiting into November.

Of the edible species mentioned in this book all but the Morels and St. George's Mushroom (see under spring) occur in the autumn though Giant Puffball and Sulphur polypore (see under summer) are past their best. A selection of typical autumn species would include: Meadow Wax Cap (*Hygrocybe pratense* p. 61), Parasol Mushroom (*Macrolepiota procera* p. 58), the Miller (*Clitopilus prunulus* p. 110), Horn of Plenty (*Craterellus cornucopioides* p. 116), Saffron Milk Cap (*Lactarius deliciosus* p. 166), Cauliflower Fungus (*Sparassis crispa* p. 174) and also the woodland Mushrooms (see pp. 105–109).

Species that rarely start before September and peak in October, or perhaps even later, include Honey Fungus (*Armillaria mellea* p. 138) and Wood Blewit (*Lepista nuda* p. 102).

Edible or Poisonous?

'To conclude, few of them are good to be eaten and most
of them do suffocate and strangle the eater.'
JOHN GERARD (1597)

WILD FUNGI ARE GATHERED AND EATEN IN PRACTICALLY EVERY PART OF THE WORLD. The origin of the practice, as with that of collecting plants for food and medicine, predates written record. Archaeological finds include South American toadstool statues from 500 BC and puffball fragments in British stone-age sites, though the latter may have been used medicinally or as tinder, rather than as food.

There are numerous accounts of fungal consumption in Roman times when the rich even employed collectors to find their favourite edible species. There are also reports of mushroom poisoning, the most infamous being the death of the Roman Emperor Claudius (10 BC–54 AD) after eating *Amanita caesarea*. This non-British species is edible and excellent but the dish was supposedly used to mask a poison, possibly from the Death Cap (*Amanita phalloides* p.151), introduced by his wife Agrippina.

For at least 3000 years herbals have named, described and illustrated plants together with information on their properties. Fungi were largely excluded, partly due to confusion as to their origin and classification. Even Linnaeus described very few fungi and classified them under the genus Chaos! In the late 16th century the herbals of Charles de l'Ecluse did include illustrations and notes on some 80 edible and poisonous fungi but British authors such as Gerard did little to enlighten the public, repeating warnings about fungi based on the 1st century AD work of Dioscorides (see quote above). The 1633 edition of Gerard's book 'The Herball', contains a drawing of Stinkhorn *(Phallus impudicus)* copied from de l'Ecluse but printed upside down! See Fig. 7.

It is therefore not surprising that references to fungi in British literature concentrate on their poisonous nature and serve to reinforce the general fear of fungi. This fear has persisted and wild fungi have not been an important part of our diet, in marked contrast to many other European countries. Possible explanations for this include the

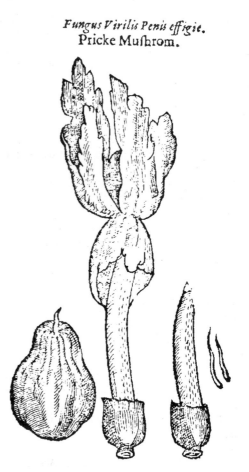

Fungus Virilis Penis effigie.
Pricke Mushrom.

*Fig. 7: An illustration from Gerard's 'The Herball' of the Stinkhorn (*Phallus impudicus*) which was reproduced upside down!*

early destruction of our woodlands, the Enclosure Acts and the long period free from war on our own territory. Ironically the entire stock of the HMSO 1940 edition of 'Edible and Poisonous Fungi' was destroyed by enemy action.

The influx into Britain, during World War II, of Poles and other refugees from fungus-friendly countries began a change in attitudes. Changes in diet (some resulting from the experience of overseas travel), together with the publication of many books on fungi aimed at the general public have resulted in many more people eating wild fungi.

Sadly, a number of earlier misconceptions still persist, for example the 'rules' that supposedly enable us to separate edible and poisonous species.

These **INACCURACIES** include:

1) The cap of an edible fungus peels easily.
2) When cooked, poisonous fungi blacken a silver spoon.
3) Salt turns yellow on the gills of poisonous fungi.
4) Species eaten by animals are safe.
5) Fungi that taste and smell pleasant are edible.
6) Bright coloured fungi are poisonous.
7) Fungi that change colour on handling, cutting or cooking are poisonous.
8) Fungi that exude a milky fluid on cutting are poisonous.
9) Cooking or drying fungi destroys any poison present.
10) All fungi collected from grassland are edible.

While all these rules appear to work in relation to a small number of species, **none of them can be relied upon** and must be regarded as dangerous superstition. A few examples of the many exceptions to the above rules will show how dangerous they are:

1) The edible Field and Horse Mushroom (*Agaricus spp*) are both easily peeled but so is the poisonous Beechwood Sickener (*Russula mairei*). See Fig. 8.

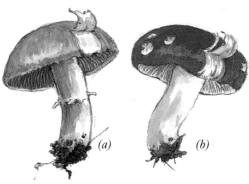

Fig. 8 (a): Edible Field Mushroom (b). Poisonous Beechwood Sickener – both can be easily peeled.

4) Slugs and insects eat a range of fungi including those that are poisonous to humans. Among mammals the rabbit can even consume the Death Cap (*Amanita phalloides*) with no ill effect. Different digestive chemicals enable some species to render fungal toxins harmless. See Fig. 9.

Fig. 9: Slug consuming Death Cap without ill-effect.

9) Some fungi such as the Blusher (*Amanita rubescens*) are poisonous when eaten raw but the poison is destroyed by the heat of cooking (see p. 19). However the toxins in the deadly Death Cap (*Amanita phalloides*) are **not** destroyed by cooking.

10) Many poisonous species are only found near trees, but among the extremely poisonous grassland species are the Ivory Clitocybe (*Clitocybe dealbata*). See Fig. 10.

Fig. 10: The deadly poisonous Ivory Clitocybe – a grassland species.

It is evident that the rules do not prevent the collection and eating of poisonous species. Equally, as some edible species are brightly coloured (e.g. many waxcaps – *Hygrocybe spp* see Fig. 11) or change colour on handling (e.g. some Boletes – *Boletus spp*), rules 6 and 7 wrongly label them as poisonous.

Fig. 11: A plate of brightly coloured, edible waxcaps.

The only safe approach to eating wild fungi is always to identify carefully and then check edibility by consulting a reliable book. Personal recommendation may not be enough as some species are enjoyed by many but poisonous to some; a good book will include this information.

Even those people who collect only a few edible species such as the Field Mushroom (*Agaricus campestris*), Chanterelle (*Cantharellus cibarius*) or Wood Blewit (*Lepista nuda*) can all too easily collect and eat a poisonous 'lookalike'. This book aims to help people to identify accurately the edible species and draws attention to any similar looking, possibly poisonous, species.

Identification is an important part of the study of natural history, but for the fungus eater it can be a matter of life or death, and if there is any doubt as to the identification of a fungus **DO NOT EAT IT**.

Edible fungi gathered in the wrong place or in the wrong condition can also cause poisoning. Fungi should not be gathered from beside busy roads, toxic waste dumps or following chemical spraying. The fruitbody may be short lived but it is nourished by the persistent mycelium and fungi are accumulators of heavy metals and even radioactive materials. Fungi collected when too old or wet, or which are kept too long before eating, may become contaminated with other fungi (moulds) and bacteria or contain toxins resulting from tissue breakdown. As with other foods, poisoning may result from this.

A matter of taste

The next section deals with fungal poisoning but first a look at what we mean by **edible**. Most larger fungi are neither poisonous nor worth eating; they are 'inedible' or 'edible but not worthwhile'. A species may be classed as edible in one book but as inedible in another – the same applies to tripe. Unfortunately the same species may be classed by one author as edible and by another as poisonous! This usually indicates a species that is poisonous unless specially prepared but may also include species that are edible to most people but upset a minority.

Edible species such as the Cep (*Boletus edulis*), Field Mushroom (*Agaricus campestris*) and Chanterelle (*Cantharellus cibarius*) would feature in most lists of species worth eating but there is considerable disagreement over others – it is a matter of personal taste. In our own selection we have drawn upon the experience of fungus eaters in Britain and from other parts of Europe to add to our own list. Legg (1990) produced a British 'Top 20'; originally based on published reports but modified in the light of readers' comments following earlier articles:

THE TOP 20 EDIBLE FUNGI IN BRITAIN
(after Legg)

1 *Boletus edulis* Cep
2 *Macrolepiota procera* Parasol Mushroom
3 *Agaricus campestris* Field Mushroom
4= *Cantharellus cibarius* Chanterelle
4= *Lepista nuda* Wood blewit
6 *Coprinus comatus* Shaggy Ink Cap
7 *Langermannia gigantea* Giant Puffball
8 *Agaricus arvensis* Horse Mushroom
9 *Xerocomus badius* Bay Bolete
10 *Lepista saeva* Field Blewit
11 *Agaricus augustus* The Prince
12= *Craterellus cornucopoides* Horn of Plenty
12= *Morchella esculenta* Morel
14 *Hydnum repandum* Hedgehog Fungus
15 *Macrolepiota rhacodes* Shaggy Parasol
16 *Russula cyanoxantha* Charcoal Burner
17= *Agaricus macrosporus* (a large Mushroom)
17= *Laetiporus sulphureus* Sulphur Polypore
19 *Calocybe gambosa* St. George's Mushroom
20 *Pleurotus ostreatus* Oyster Mushroom

Such a list is of course affected by the availability of species and ease of identification. The highly prized Truffle is not on the list because it is so rarely found in Britain, but we have included it in this book. From our own experience we would add:

Sparassis crispa Cauliflower Fungus
Leccinum versipelle Orange Birch Bolete
Clitopilus prunulus The Miller
Hygrocybe pratensis Meadow Wax Cap

We are also aware that two of the species listed may upset some people and for this reason advise caution with:

Macrolepiota rhacodes Shaggy Parasol
Laetiporus sulphureus Sulphur Polypore

In this book we have included some edible *Amanita* species such as the Blusher and the Grisette in a poisonous section because they are too easily confused by beginners with deadly *Amanita* species. The Common Ink Cap (*Coprinus atramentarius*) is also included in the section on poisonous species found in grassland areas because of its effects when consumed with alcohol.

All the top 20 are included in the book but we have not ranked their culinary properties as we believe it pre-judges the issue and some advice is best taken with a pinch of salt – this is likely to improve the flavour!

THE MOST POISONOUS FUNGI IN BRITAIN
include:

Amanita pantherina Panther Cap
Amanita phalloides Death Cap
Amanita virosa Destroying Angel
Claviceps purpurea Ergot
Clitocybe dealbata Ivory Clitocybe
Clitocybe rivulosa
Cortinarius speciosissimus
Entoloma lividum Livid Entoloma
Galerina marginata
Gyromitra esculenta Turban Fungus
Inocybe patouillardii Red-staining Inocybe
Lepiota cristata Stinking Parasol

In this book all the above are referred to in cases where they can be confused with edible species, and the common ones are more fully described in the relevant sections concerned with poisonous species.

Fungus Poisoning

FUNGI COMMONLY PRODUCE A WIDE RANGE OF COMPLEX CHEMICALS, some of which are poisonous to animals, including humans. Such poisons can be divided into two categories. When they are produced by mould that contaminate food, they are referred to as mycotoxins, and may cause illness or death in extreme cases. A different range of toxins is found in the fruitbodies of certain mushrooms and toadstools. There are few species which cause fatal poisoning, but some give rise to unpleasant symptoms.

We have followed the excellent booklet *Wild Mushroom and Toadstool Poisoning* by Oldridge, Pegler and Spooner in recognising the following categories of fungal toxins. Broadly speaking they range from the most to the least poisonous.

1. CYTOLYTIC TOXINS

Cytolytic (cyto = cell, lytic = destroying) toxins attack certain body tissues. They are selective in their targets, and attack the cells of the liver and kidney in particular. Three main groups of cytotoxins have been recognised: cyclopetides, orellanin and gyromytrin.

(a) Cyclopeptides

Cyclopeptides are molecules made up from either seven or eight amino acids linked in the form of a ring. In nature the cyclopeptides are probably bound on to carbohydrates to form extremely large molecules called myriaminins. These appear to be broken down in the digestive system to release their cyclopeptides, which enter the blood stream and are carried to the liver and kidneys where they attack the cells, causing irreversible failure of both organs.

Poisoning by cyclopeptides is most commonly associated with consumption of species of *Amanita*, particularly *A. phalloides* (Death Cap). Other species, such as *A. virosa* (Destroying Angel), also contain large quantities, but are rare in Britain and so seldom cause a problem. Cyclopeptides also occur in other genera, for example *Lepiota castanea*, *Galerina marginata* and *Conocybe filaris*.

Consumption of *Amanita phalloides* is typically

*Fig. 12: Death Cap (*Amanita phalloides*)*

followed by the onset of vomiting and diarrhoea after 6–24 hours, resulting in dehydration and a fall in blood pressure and blood sugar level. There may then be a remission of these symptoms for several days. However, during this remission the cyclopeptides cause progressive damage to the liver and kidneys, leading to collapse and coma, followed eventually by death.

There have been many attempts to devise treatments for cyclopeptide poisoning. Some of these

18

have been effective when taken shortly after consumption of the fungus, and in 1981 Dr Pierre Bastien successfully tested on himself a mixture containing anti-diarrhoeals, antibiotics and Vitamin C. Thioctic acid and activated charcoal have also been used. However such treatments are often administered too late due to the patient's apparent recovery from the initial symptoms and consequent failure to seek medical advice.

(b) Orellanin

Orellanin is the collective name for a group of compounds first described from *Cortinarius orellanus* which attack the cells of the kidneys. These toxins are stable even when the fruitbodies have been cooked or dried.

There is typically a delay of 36–48 hours between consumption and the onset of symptoms. These include gastro-enteric disorders followed by head- and muscle-ache and back pain. Kidney failure occurs between one and three weeks after eating the fungus and usually proves fatal. The only treatment for orellanin poisoning that has proved effective in some cases is kidney dialysis.

Cortinarius orellanus is a species of beech wood with a southern-based distribution in Europe, and hence is rather rare in Britain. However the related, and equally poisonous, *C. speciosissimus* has been collected in Scottish coniferous woodland and eaten in error for the Chanterelle. Some other species of *Cortinarius* also contain orellanin.

(c) Gyromytrin

Gyromytrin occurs in the False Morel or Turban Fungus (*Gyromitra esculenta*). Consumption of the raw fruitbody causes poisoning but the toxin is broken down by heating above 60°C, rendering the fungus edible. In continental Europe it has traditionally been prepared by boiling twice in water which is then discarded. However it is extremely unwise to eat *Gyromitra* as it also contains carcinogenic hydrazines.

Gyromytrin is broken down in the acid conditions of the stomach to the toxic monomethyl hydrazine. After a delay of 6–10 hours there is an onset of sickness and headache, followed by jaundice, coma and in some cases death.

Old specimens of Morel (*Morchella* spp) may occasionally cause similar symptoms. Gyromytrin poisoning is treated by large doses of intravenous pyridoxine, administered under medical supervision.

2. HAEMOLYTIC TOXINS

*Fig. 13: The Blusher (*Amanita rubescens*)*

Haemolytic (haem = blood) toxins attack red blood cells, thereby giving rise to anaemia. There is usually a delay of several hours before symptoms begin to appear. These include pallor and blockage of the kidneys in rare cases. Two species that commonly cause problems are the Blusher (*Amanita rubescens*) and the Grisette (*Amanita vaginata*) but, as haemolytic toxins are broken down by heat, thorough cooking generally renders them safe enough to eat.

There are three main groups of toxins that have their primary effect on the central nervous system, altering both perception and the control of bodily function. Symptoms usually develop within an hour and commonly include hallucination and delirium.

(a) Isoxazole derivatives

Fly Agaric (*Amanita muscaria*) and Panther Cap (*Amanita pantherina*) contain several compounds such as muscimol, muscazone and ibotenic acid. These induce activity of the central nervous system and may give rise to hallucinations. Because of this Fly Agaric has been used ritualistically in a number of cultures (see p. 34).

*Fig. 14: Comon Ink Cap (*Coprinus atramentarius*)*

Coprine is an amino acid found in some species of Ink Cap(*Coprinus*), particularly Common Ink Cap (*C. atramentarius*). Coprine is broken down in the body to aminocyclopropanol, which prevents the action of an enzyme responsible for breaking down acetaldehyde. Normally there is very little acetaldehyde in the body, so that the inactivity of this enzyme poses no problem. However, when alcohol is consumed, it is converted to acetaldehyde which accumulates if the enzyme is inactive. If alcohol is drunk within 48 hours of eating Coprine, symptoms may develop within ten minutes. These include a metallic taste, blushing, palpitation, chest pain, vomiting and diarrhoea.

Coprine has been positively identified in *Coprinus atramentarius*, but may well also occur in the related *C. acuminatus* and *C. romagnesianus*. Other species that produce similar symptoms include Shaggy Pholiota (*Pholiota squarrosa*), Lurid Bolete (*Boletus luridus*), Club-footed Funnel Cap (*Clitocybe clavipes*) and *Tricholoma flavovirens*.

*Fig. 15: Liberty Cap (*Philocybe semilanceata*)*

(b) Indole compounds

Psilocin and psilocybin are indole compounds found in Liberty Cap (*Psilocybe semilanceata*) and several other species in the same family, for example Hoop Petticoat Fungus (*Panaeolus sphinctrinus*) and Brown Hay Cap (*Panaeolina foenisecii*). These compounds stimulate perception, producing symptoms similar to alcohol intoxication – dilation of pupils, rapid breathing, lowered body temperature and increased blood pressure – that persist for several hours. 'Flashbacks' can occur for some months in certain cases.

(c) Alkaloids

Some bracket fungi, such as the Giant Polypore (*Meripilus giganteus*) and Sulphur Polypore (*Laetiporus sulphureus*) contain hordenine, tyramine and methyltyramine which may cause dizziness and disorientation, possibly with sickness and gastro-enteric discomfort. Individuals seem to vary in their susceptibility to this type of poisoning.

---

5. MUSCARINE POISONING

*Fig. 16: Fly Agaric (*Amanita muscaria*)*

Muscarine is an alkaloid and the first fungal toxin to be characterised. It was originally isolated from Fly Agaric (*Amanita muscaria*), but is present in only small quantities in that species. Symptoms usually develop after about 15 minutes and include stimulation of the secretory glands causing profuse sweating, salivation and weeping. There may also

be nausea, vomiting, diarrhoea, and blurred vision. Atropine is a specific antidote to muscarine; 1 mg injected under medical supervision rapidly reverses the symptoms.

*Fig. 17: Panther Cap (*Amanita pantherina*)*

Species of mushroom that contain dangerous amounts of muscarine include Panther Cap (*Amanita pantherina*), Ivory or Sweating Mushroom (*Clitocybe dealbata*), *C. rivulosa*, Red-staining Inocybe, (*Inocybe patouillardii*), *I. fastigiata*, *I. geophylla* and Jack O'Lantern (*Omphalotus olearius*). Small quantities are found in the Bell Caps (*Mycena pura* and *M. rosea*) and also in *Omphalina ericetorum*.

Fig. 18: Inocybe geophylla var. lilacina

6. Gastro-enteric poisons

A large number of fungi exert their principal effect on the digestive tract. They range from those causing severe poisoning to those that provoke a minor stomach upset. Usually the chemical basis for such poisoning is not known and there are no specific antidotes. Symptoms include vomiting, abdominal pain and stomach cramp. Particularly severe effects are produced by three species:

*Fig. 19 Brown Roll-rim (*Paxillus involutus*)*

Brown Roll-Rim (*Paxillus involutus*) has a history of having been eaten in eastern Europe but can cause severe, or even fatal, poisoning. Repeated consumption may lead to cumulative poisoning and death.

Livid Entoloma (*Entoloma lividum*) causes severe symptoms, including stomach cramp. There may also be fatal liver damage. *Entoloma rhodopolium* and *E. nidorosum* produce similar symptoms but are less toxic.

Sulphur Tuft (*Hypholoma fasciculare*) causes digestive upsets, and in some cases may cause liver damage.

Other species cause less acute symptoms and are very unlikely to be fatal. However, their effects are unpleasant and they should be avoided. They include:

Yellow-staining Mushroom (*Agaricus xanthodermus*).
Devil's Bolete (*Boletus satanus*), Peppery Bolete (*B. piperatus*), *B. calopus* and Bitter Bolete (*Tylopilus felleus*) – particularly if eaten raw.
Poison Pie (*Hebeloma crustuliniforme*).
Silky Nolanea (*Nolanea sericea*) and related species.
Several species of Milk Cap including Peppery (*Lactarius piperatus*), Rufous (L. *rufus*), Woolly (L. *torminosus*), Ugly (L. *turpis*) and *helvus*.
Several species of *Russula* including The Sickener (*Russula emetica*), *R. sanguinea*, *R. Mairei* and *R. foetens*.
The Earthballs – *Scleroderma citrinum* and *verrucosum*.
Tricholoma species including *T. saponaceum*, *T. sulphureum* and T. *ustale*.

In addition to these species there are some that are commonly eaten throughout Europe but which occasionally cause digestive upsets, e.g. Weeping Widow (*Lacrymaria velutina*) and Honey Fungus (*Armillaria mellea*). It may be that individuals differ in their sensitivity to these species, or that different collections of them vary in their toxicity. In the case of the Honey Fungus, for example, what was once considered to be a single species has since been shown to comprise at least three (*A. mellea, bulbosa* and *ostoyae*) which differ in their morphology and ecology. It is possible that they differ also in their edibility.

There are no specific antidotes for gastro-enteric poisoning, but various treatments can be tried. If the patient has not vomited, they should be encouraged to do so in order to remove the fungus from the digestive tract. However there is usually excessive vomiting and diarrhoea which may lead to dehydration, so the patient should drink plenty of liquid. Drugs may be administered under medical supervision to control excessive sickness. Activated charcoal will control the uptake of poisons from the digestive tract.

7. ALLERGIES

Edible fungi can cause allergic reactions in certain individuals in just the same way that many other foods can. A wide range of symptoms may develop, including digestive upsets, headaches and nettle-rash. If a large amount has been eaten, the reaction may be very unpleasant. If you have a tendency to allergic reaction, it is sensible to limit portion size when first sampling wild mushrooms. Species to which some people are known to react include Clouded Agaric (*Clitocybe nebularis*), Wood Blewit (*Lepista nuda*) and Shaggy Parasol (*Macrolepiota rhacodes*).

Some people also develop allergic reactions if they inhale fungal spores, for example of Oyster Mushroom (*Pleurotus ostreatus*), and Puffball spores may cause inflammation of the eye. Occasionally, very sensitive individuals may develop contact dermatitis when they handle certain species of mushroom.

8. IMAGINARY POISONING

The fear of fungal poisoning is widespread and for this reason some people will not eat any species, even cultivated ones. Those who are persuaded to eat wild fungi may not be convinced that they are safe. Fear alone can cause some people to experience symptoms including stomach-ache and diarrhoea, but the only long-term effect is increased fungal phobia.

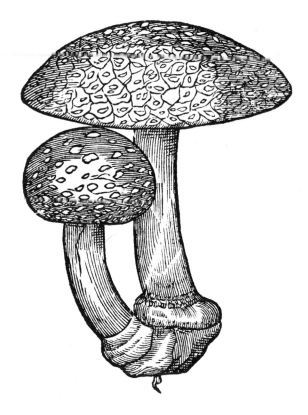

Conservation

WE ARE FAMILIAR WITH THE IDEA OF PROTECTING ANIMALS AND PLANTS but, until very recently, little consideration has been given to the need for fungal conservation. In 1989 the European Council for the Conservation of Fungi was established up to coordinate the efforts of national groups such as the British Mycological Society.

The decline of fungi

Throughout Europe there is evidence that fungi are declining in both variety and numbers. In Holland, for example, a national recording and mapping scheme provides accurate information about changes in the status of fungi. Mycorrhizal species and those with specialised habitats have suffered the most dramatic reductions. Decline appears to be the result of several factors. Loss of habitats inevitably reduces the range of sites at which fungi can grow; losses result from agricultural improvement or changes in management and land use.

Pollution

Even when management is maintained, sites may decline in value because of pollution. One of the major culprits is atmospheric sulphur dioxide (SO_2) which has caused serious decline in European forests. Another group of pollutants is nitrogen compounds, which appear to be particularly important in Holland. Mushroom picking is not regarded as an important factor in the decline of fungi other than in Poland, where concern has been expressed about intensive commercial picking of edible species.

Fungal conservation

It is most important to know which species are most at risk, both in a European context and within Britain. The British Mycological Society has published a provisional *Red Data List of British Fungi* (Ing, 1992) that includes 583 species. These range from rare species that are not at present threatened, through those considered to be particularly vulnerable, to those which are either extinct or threatened with extinction in the near future. Having this checklist will help biologists to assess the importance of a particular site for fungi.

Conservation of fungi is something that can be achieved in isolation. Fungi are intimately associated with other organisms in the ecosystem, so that successful conservation must involve the management of a site as a functioning whole. However it is possible to take the needs of fungi into account when designing a management scheme for a site. In woodland dying or dead standing trees provide important habitats for fungi, as do their fallen branches and trunks. Among the edible fungi Oyster Mushroom (*Pleurotus ostreatus*), Branded Oyster Mushroom (*P. cornucopiae*) and Velvet Shank (*Flammulina velutipes*) have all benefited from the wealth of dead standing elm trunks left by Dutch Elm disease. It is good conservation practice to leave dead wood to decay in situ.

Not all sites that support an interesting and diverse community of fungi are necessarily of great interest to those concerned with plant or animal conservation. Beech (*Fagus sylvatica*) woods are unlikely to cause a stir in the heart of many botanists; on the one hand they tend to shade out most other species and on the other the beech is not a native species throughout most of the British Isles. Yet a beech wood can be one of the most productive habitats for fungi. Similarly in the north of England large tracts of hill country have been devoted to sheep grazing. These nutrient-poor acid grasslands are not 'natural' vegetation and support an unremarkable range of plants, but in the autumn there is a dramatic fruiting of fungi in the short sheep-grazed turf.

Preserving Fungi

THE CALENDAR ON PP. 11–13 SHOWS THAT IT IS POSSIBLE TO FIND EDIBLE SPECIES in high summer and even in the depths of winter, but the main flush is in the autumn and some highly prized species have a short fruiting season. Such species can be enjoyed throughout the year by using a variety of preserving techniques; some of which even enhance aroma and taste. A few species can be bought dried or pickled, but at a high price.

Refrigeration
With the exception of the Ink Caps most fungi will keep in a refrigerator for a few days, provided they are collected young, dry and insect-free. Do not store them in a plastic bag.

Freezing
Fungi are easy to freeze but the thawed results can be disappointing. The Mushrooms (*Agaricus spp*) and the Boletes freeze well raw. Loose-freeze small specimens on a tray before packing them in airtight bags. Slicing and blanching (in boiling water for three minutes then into cold water) before freezing extends the shelf-life but raw mushrooms should not be kept frozen for more than a year. Do **not** thaw out before cooking unless you like eating slugs or rubber! Carluccio (1989) recommends either deep frying the frozen mushrooms for a few seconds or boiling in salted water for a few minutes, before cooking as if fresh.

Duxelles can be prepared from many species (even mixtures) by chopping finely with onion, salt and pepper and sautéing in butter before freezing. Add to stock for soups or sauces.

Drying
This is the cheapest method and many dried fungi are unusual in that they maintain the qualities of the fresh material when reconstituted with water. This is largely due to the properties of the fungal sugar trehalose, which is currently being tested as an additive to other dried foods where it enhances flavour and texture (Roser and Colaco 1993).

Fresh fungi contain up to 90% water so only those with a firm texture respond well to drying. Use young, non-maggoty specimens and do not wash them – brush them or cut away dirt. Small ones can be dried whole, larger ones need cutting into cubes 1–2 cm square. Thread the pieces onto string or wire like a kebab (but with the pieces separated) and place above a radiator or in an airing cupboard. See Fig. 20.

Fig. 20: Drying pieces of Cep above a radiator.

When completely dry, store in airtight containers – this keeps the moisture out and the smell in. Well-dried fungi will keep for years. To reconstitute soak in warm water (or wine) for 15–30 minutes and use the liquid as stock. In some fungi, as with certain herbs, the aroma is increased on drying and the resulting dried material can be ground to a powder using a coffee mill or food processor. This can even be used to augment the flavour of a fresh mushroom dish.

Among those species that reconstitute well from the dried state are: Cep (*Boletus edulis*), Bay Bolete (*Xerocomus badius*), Orange Birch Bolete (*Leccinum versipelle*), Slippery Jack (*Suillus luteus*) – after discarding the sticky layer, the Morels (*Morchella spp*), Horn of Plenty (*Craterellus cornucopoides*), Fairy Ring Champignon (*Marasmius oreades*) and Jew's Ear (*Auricularia auricula-judae*).

Pickling

Pickling maintains much of the texture and colour but adds a sharp flavour. Use only young, firm, clean specimens and very clean, sterilised screw-top jars. For 1/2 kg of fungi you will require 250 ml wine vinegar diluted with 100 ml water, 2 teaspoons of salt, a bay leaf and spices to personal taste (e.g. clove, peppercorn, marjoram). Boil the fungi in the mixture for about 5 minutes before draining, allow to cool and put in sterilised jars filled up with cold olive oil. More traditional methods involve cooking and pickling in the vinegar – this keeps longer but imparts a sharper taste. Once opened, the contents must be refrigerated and used within a few days.

Preserving in Alcohol

Peaches keep well in brandy and so do fungi – always remembering that some species produce violent symptoms with alcohol (see p. 20). It works best for small fruitbodies which can be preserved whole after first blanching in an alcohol such as vermouth. (Beware – boiling alcohol can catch fire). For the preservative use brandy or any suitable liqueur.

Mushroom Ketchup

Slice the mushrooms (and here older specimens can be used) and simmer in a little water with plenty of salt to draw out the liquid. Squeeze out the liquid, discard the solids and then add more salt, black pepper, cloves, cinnamon, bay leaves and mustard seed to the liquid which should then be boiled until it thickens. Strain into a bottle (older recipes add some port at this stage) and store in a refrigerator.

Fig. 21: Brush away any dirt; do not wash

Fig. 22: Frying thinly sliced wild mushrooms

Cooking Fungi

If your Lord or Lady loves not Oyle,
Stewe them with a Little Sweete Butter
and a little White Wine.
(ANON, 17TH CENTURY)

SEVERAL BOOKS HAVE BEEN PUBLISHED ON THE SUBJECT OF COOKING FUNGI (e.g. Grigson 1975 and Carluccio 1989) and though they have included descriptions of edible (and a few poisonous) species, these have been secondary to the culinary information. This book concentrates on the identification of a wider range of edible species (and of important poisonous ones) and is not intended as a recipe book. Notes on cooking are given with the individual species information; what follows is some general advice about preparing and cooking wild fungi.

Preparation

Before eating any fungus double-check its identity; it is all too easy to collect a poisonous lookalike together with, or in error for, an edible species. If you have several species, keep them separate as they may require different cooking methods. Discard those that are obviously too old – they maybe soggy, very maggot infected or have a musty smell indicative of mould infection. Clean the rest using a small brush or by cutting away very soiled areas. See Fig. 21. If necessary use a damp cloth but do not wash them – their water content is high enough. Peeling is only required if the skin is slimy or very tough. Unless you require small whole fungi for pickling, or larger ones for stuffing, it is useful to remove the stem and quarter the cap – this aids cleaning and allows a detailed maggot inspection. Do not remove gills or tubes unless they are damaged or are very wet, but do discard tough stems.

Cooking, digestibility and flavour are all enhanced by using thin slices. See Fig. 22. Once prepared, fungi should be cooked and eaten without delay.

Cooking

The basic method is to fry the fungi in butter, oil or an oil-based margarine over a medium heat for about four minutes. Fill and empty the pan quickly – this avoids under- or over-cooking part of the collection. Too high a heat means the fat will burn and the fungi will not be cooked throughout; too long at low heat results in excessive water. Overcooking makes some fungi chewy and tasteless.

If too much water is exuded this should be drained off for use in a sauce; salt increases exudation so is best added late, together with a dash of lemon juice to enhance flavour. Experiment with adding herbs and spices such as pepper, fresh parsley, or garlic. Remember that some species have a subtle flavour which should not be masked.

For extra flavour or a different texture add wine, cream or yoghurt just before serving. Coat larger pieces (Parasol caps or Puffball slices for instance) with egg or milk and cover with breadcrumbs or porridge oats before frying until golden brown. Large firm species (including Boletes, Mushrooms, Puffballs and some Brackets) can be grilled or stuffed and baked in the oven.

For soups and sauces where plenty of liquid and a soft texture is required, cut the fungi into small pieces and sauté on a low heat. Young firm fungi can be eaten raw in salads but apart from small amounts of Mushrooms (*Agaricus spp*) and Chanterelle (*Cantharellus cibarius*) we do not recommend it. Many fungi are difficult to digest raw and more seriously some have poisons that are only destroyed by the heat of cooking.

Enjoy eating fungi but do not eat large quantities at a time (100 g/4 oz is sufficient). If you are trying something for the first time eat a small amount and do not mix it with other novel foods. Bon appetit!

The Food Value of Fungi

IN PARTS OF NORTHERN AND EASTERN EUROPE dried and pickled wild fungi have been important substitutes for vegetables in winter and for meat during times of shortage or when religious rites forbade the consumption of flesh. Despite this there is considerable disagreement as to the true nutritional value of fungi.

Relatively little work has been done on wild fungi but there is considerable variation between species and between different developmental stages of the same species. Substratum plays an important role in the mineral content of fungi (see p. 37).

1) Fresh fungi contain about 90% water, comparable to many vegetables. (Air-dried fungi contain about 10% water.)

2) Fat content varies from 2–8% of the dry weight – in Cultivated Mushroom (*Agaricus bisporus*) for example, this is mostly linoleic acid (an unsaturated fat).

3) Carbohydrates make up over 50% of the dry weight and include glucose, sucrose and trehalose ('mushroom sugar') – the latter found mainly in young fruitbodies. Much of the carbohydrate is in the form of chitin which is the structural component of the fungus mycelium. This contributes to the high fibre content of fungi but can make them difficult to digest.

4) Fungi contain about 35 kilocalories per 100 g, comparable to many vegetables.

5) Fungi provide appreciable amounts of vitamins though there is considerable variation between species. The B vitamins (thiamine, niacin and riboflavin) are the most common, together with ergosterol, the precursor of vitamin D. The provitamin carotene is found in some Boletes and in Chanterelle (*Cantharellus cibarius*). Mushrooms are a good source of folic acid (which significantly reduces the incidence of babies born with neural tube defects).

6) The mineral content of fungi includes phosphorus and potassium together with trace elements such as copper (essential for red blood cells) and selenium (currently being investigated for its role in preventing cancers).

The main area of disagreement is over the amount and value of fungal protein. Early studies indicated a figure of over 5% of the dry weight. This put fungi between vegetables and meat in terms of their protein value. More recent work has shown that the essential amino acid component and digestibility of the protein are important in determining nutritive value, and that this varies considerably between species. Crisan and Sands (1978) concluded that certain species (including the commercial Mushroom) were comparable to foods such as milk but others were 'singularly undistinguished in their nutritional contribution to diet'.

Commercially grown fungi take up very little growing space compared with some other high protein foods. Cooke (1977) calculated that the amount of protein produced per hectare per year is 65, 000 kg for mushrooms, compared with 78 kg for beef cattle. An even higher production of fungal protein can be achieved by the continuous culture of lower fungi such as *Fusarium graminearum* in which the vegetative hyphae are harvested, processed and sold as the myco-protein Quorn. This has a protein content between that of beef sausage and cod and with its high-fibre, low-fat and nil-cholesterol content is marketed as a health food. Fungi are increasingly seen as part of a healthy diet, which may explain the increased consumption of commercially grown mushrooms (see next section) and a booming interest in edible wild species.

Mushroom Cultivation

ALTHOUGH IT IS POSSIBLE TO FIND WILD EDIBLE MUSHROOMS throughout the year, the supply of most individual species is markedly seasonal (see pp. 11–13). Fruiting depends upon temperature and rainfall, so the supply may fluctuate markedly from year to year. Field mushrooms are a good example; heavy crops tend to follow rain in years when there has been a hot dry summer.

In order to control some of this variation there have been many attempts to bring different species into cultivation. The grower can then try to provide those conditions that will favour regular heavy cropping. Most success has been achieved with decomposer fungi which can be inoculated on to a suitable growing medium, but more recently growers have managed to cultivate mycorrhizal fungi such as Truffles.

*Fig. 23: Cultivated Mushroom (*Agaricus bisporus*) in trays of compost.*

Decomposer fungi can be grown on a wide range of substrata, depending on the ecology of the species in the wild. The cultivated European Mushroom (*Agaricus bisporus*) was originally collected from meadows in which horses grazed or from heaps of horse-dung around stables; it is traditionally cultivated on compost based on horse-dung. Similarly the oriental Padi-straw Mushroom (*Volvariella volvacea*) is traditionally grown on composted rice straw. Another oriental mushroom, Shiitake (*Lentinellus edodes*), by contrast, is a wood-rotting species which is traditionally cultivated on logs of oak or chestnut in Japan.

The cultivation of *Agaricus bisporus* in Europe can be traced back to the late 17th century. Horse manure from stables was stacked in underground caves below Paris and inoculated with soil from sites where the mushroom grew wild. The cool conditions in the caves favoured fruiting. Cultivation of mushrooms as a delicacy for aristocratic tables spread throughout Europe in the 18th and 19th centuries, but it was not until the 20th century that improved techniques allowed production of cheap mushrooms throughout the year.

Fig. 24: Vertical section through a mushroom bed showing fruitbodies on the casing layer.

The first step in modern cultivation is the preparation of the growing medium. Mushrooms are grown on a compost of straw, which provides their carbon, and animal dung, which provides their nitrogen. Although horse-dung was originally used, some growers use chicken manure instead, as it is more readily available and more consistent. When the straw and dung have been thoroughly mixed the compost is stacked.

Microbial activity in the stack causes the temperature to rise to about 60°C and changes the chemical and physical characteristics of the compost. In particular the ratio between carbon and nitrogen (C:N ratio) falls to about 17:1 as carbon is lost by microbial respiration. Several microbial products accumulate, such as protein, dextrins and acetate which are all important nutrients for subsequent mushroom growth.

The finished compost has very few readily-available soluble nutrients in it, as these have been taken up by the microbes. This is important, as it prevents further microbial activity and the growth of weed fungi that might compete with *Agaricus*. The compost is transferred to a Pasteurising chamber where it is held at 70°C for up to 12 hours to complete the composting process.

The compost is then transferred carefully to growing rooms, avoiding contamination by pests that would interfere with mushroom growth. The compost is mixed with inoculum (spawn) of *Agaricus bisporus* growing on grain and spread into trays or shelves to a depth of about 25 cm. The growing house is kept at a temperature of 25°C for about 14 days while the mycelium colonises the compost. Then a 'casing' layer is spread over the surface of the compost. In the UK this is usually peat, made neutral with ground limestone. The casing contains no nutrients that *Agaricus* can use, but the mycelium grows up into it from the compost below and the resulting crop is much cleaner.

Seven days after casing the temperature in the house is reduced to between 14°C and 18°C and the CO_2 concentration to below 0.1%. The lack of nutrients in the casing and the reduced temperature subject the fungus to stress which initiates the growth of young fruitbodies (primordia). The first crop (or 'flush') of mature mushrooms is picked about 14 days later. The bed will produce perhaps six further flushes at weekly intervals before it is no longer economic to pick the mushrooms. The spent compost is then emptied from the growing house, which is sterilised to control pests and disease before being refilled for the next growing cycle.

Shiitake (*Lentinellus edodes*) was originally collected from the wild, probably by the Chinese. Documents record its being offered to the Emperor Chuai of Japan in 199 AD. It occurs naturally on the dead wood of oaks, chestnuts and hornbeams. Early attempts to encourage its growth involved cutting small notches on dead trunks to allow natural inoculation by spores in the air. By the late 19th century growers had started to inoculate wood deliberately.

In Japan living trees are felled in the autumn at a time when the wood has a relatively high sugar content. The trunks are left for one or two months to allow cell death and a lowering of the natural defence reactions of the wood, and are then sawn into logs about 1 m long. The logs are inoculated by drilling holes and filling them with *Lentinellus* inoculum. The inoculated logs are stacked

*Fig. 25: Shiitake (*Lentinellus edodes*) fruiting on logs in a raising yard.*

obliquely in a 'laying yard', traditionally under light woodland shade but more commonly under plastic shading now.

The logs remain in the laying yard for about 18 months while the mycelium colonises the wood, growth being optimal around 25°c. The fully colonised logs are transferred, usually during winter, to a 'raising yard', where they are leaned up against supports. Fruiting starts in spring when the temperature is between 12°C and 20°C; it requires high humidity, so the logs are watered and the yard kept well shaded. Logs should continue to produce crops in spring and autumn for between three and six years. The picked mushrooms can either be used fresh, or more commonly are dried.

Japanese growers have succeeded in cultivating other edible mushrooms, such as the Velvet-shank (*Flammulina velutipes*), on sawdust. Western growers have adapted this technique for cultivation of both Shiitake and Oyster Mushroom (*Pleurotus ostreatus*). Sawdust is packed into plastic bags, heat-sterilised and then inoculated. When the sawdust is fully colonised the plastic can be peeled off as the mycelium holds the sawdust together. The temperature is reduced and fruitbodies develop on the surface of the sawdust.

Cultivation of mycorrhizal fungi has proved much more difficult than that of decomposer species, since the grower has to establish and maintain a delicate relationship between two organisms, the fungus and its tree partner. The most successful attempt to achieve this has been the establishment of plantations ('truffieres') for the production of black truffles (*Tuber melanosporum*). French and Italian scientists developed techniques in the 1970s for inoculating oak and hazel seedlings with black truffle mycelium. Infected plants are grown in special nurseries and are sold to growers wishing to establish plantations. Truffieres have also been established in New Zealand, producing their first (few!) truffles in 1993.

There has been increasing interest in small-scale cultivation under domestic conditions. Several commercial compost producers now supply spawned mushroom compost in plastic bags that can be incubated at home to produce flushes of *Agaricus bisporus*. Specialist growers supply bags of growing medium which have been inoculated with one of the variously coloured species of Oyster Mushroom, for example grey *Pleurotus ostreatus*, yellow *P. citrinopileatus* and pink *P. salmoneostramineus*. It is also possible to buy artificial 'logs' which have been inoculated with Shiitake.

The two of us tend to rely on finding and gathering wild mushrooms rather than having to cultivate them, but one of us unintentionally succeeded in growing Wood Blewits (*Lepista nuda*) on garden compost. Some discarded pieces of Blewit were thrown on to the heap one autumn; the compost went into the greenhouse the following summer and yielded an unexpected mixed crop of tomatoes and Blewits!

Fungal Folklore – Fact and Fiction

GIVEN THE SUDDEN APPEARANCE (SEEMINGLY OUT OF NOTHING) and ephemeral nature of many fungi, coupled with their poisonous reputation, it is not surprising that they occupy a prominent place in myth and folklore. Fungi were often associated with fairies, elves and witches – the latter being held responsible for distributing the Witchs' Eggs that 'hatched' into the penis-like Stinkhorn (*Phallus impudicus*). Among common names for fungi we find Witches Butter, Fairies Bonnets and the Orange Elf-cup.

FAIRY RINGS

The association with fairies was widely held as the explanation for the appearance of toadstools in 'fairy rings'. In grassland habitats rings of darker green grass foretell the position of the fruitbodies and are often accompanied by a band of short dead grass – like a diminutive race track. Other explanations included the work of moles, tethered goats and the effects of lightening! The recent plethora of crop circles and speculation as to their origin is strangely similar.

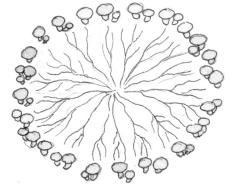

Fig. 26: Fruitbody production near the margin of the expanding mycelium.

Fig. 26 shows the scientific explanation, with the fruitbodies developing near the margin of the ever-expanding fungal mycelium, just as a tree produces flowers near the branch ends. The circular growth of a fungus is easily seen in the moulds; and among the higher fungi the most regular rings are found on lawns and playing fields where the carefully prepared soil ensures unimpeded growth.

Fig. 27 explains the fertilising effect on grass at the growing front (caused by increased availability of soil nutrients resulting from the action of fungal enzymes) and diminished growth further back due to depletion of nutrients, lack of aeration and possible production of fungal toxins)

The realisation that an expanding fairy ring represented one individual fungus helped debunk another myth – that fungi are ephemeral. Aerial photography has revealed huge rings which must result from growth over many centuries. Recent developments in DNA testing (comparable to genetic fingerprinting in humans) have detected a single genetic individual of Honey Fungus (*Armillaria bulbosa*) covering 15 hectares of a Michigan forest. Smith (1992) and his colleagues measured the vegetative growth of the fungus and concluded that it must be some 1500 years old. While the fruitbody may be ephemeral the underlying mycelium is closer to being eternal.

Fig. 27: Cross-section through a grassland fairy ring.

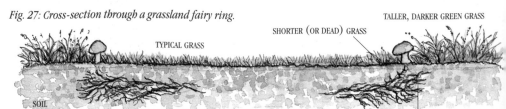

TALLER, DARKER GREEN GRASS

SHORTER (OR DEAD) GRASS

TYPICAL GRASS

SOIL

ADVANCING MARGIN OF FUNGAL MYCELIUM

ERGOTISM: FROM HOLY FIRE TO THE SALEM WITCH TRIALS

Ergot (*Claviceps purpurea*), described on p. 75, may be small in stature but it has caused immense suffering and has been responsible for a considerable body of folklore. The link between the disease now known as ergotism and the eating of flour ground from grain (principally rye) infected with ergot was not proven until 1785 but there are numerous accounts of the disease in Europe from as early as the 9th century.

The rye growing regions of France, Germany and Russia chronicled symptoms including unquenchable thirst, a burning sensation, tingling and itching of the skin, gangrene leading to loss of limbs, blindness, loss of milk in nursing mothers, fertility suppression, muscle spasm, hallucinations and psychosis. There were many deaths, particularly among children.

From the 12th century those afflicted in France sought help from the order of St Anthony. Anthony had lived in Egypt during the 3rd century and developed a reputation for having power over fire. The burning sensation, earlier dubbed the Holy Fire, became known as St. Anthony's Fire.

A fascinating study by Mary Matossian (1989) seeks to link the effects of ergotism with the 15th century population decline in northwestern Europe. This was a time of cold winters and wet summers; conditions that encourage the growth of ergot. Late medieval Europe also saw an increase in court cases of witchcraft accusations. The spasms and hallucinations of ergotism were frequently attributed to witchcraft. Matossian found a close correlation between incidences of 16th- and 17th-century witchcraft trials and poor summers (calculated from tree ring widths) in regions where rye was the staple food.

Ergot is not restricted to Europe, and Matossian suggests that the symptoms of the Salem children that led to the famous witch trials in 1692 were caused by convulsive ergotism following a cool, moist year. The staple crop of New England at that time was rye.

Central Europe saw a decline in ergotism from the end of the 18th century, due to a decrease in the acreage of rye (being replaced by potatoes and wheat), and to the introduction of methods to separate the diseased grain. Russia however was still suffering thousands of outbreaks in the 1920s and the Ethiopian famine resulted in ergot deaths in 1977, when infected grass seed was used as food.

The development of resistant strains of rye and the spraying of fungicides have virtually banished ergotism from the developed countries. Despite this, ergot is still very common on wild grasses and its effects on cattle and sheep are significant, though difficult to quantify.

HALLUCINOGENIC FUNGI

The chemicals responsible for the symptoms of ergotism are a group of alkaloids, many of which are based on the lysergic acid molecule. In 1938 Dr Albert Hofmann was working on derivatives of the ergot alkaloids in the search for novel medicinal drugs. He synthesised *d*-lysergic acid diethylamide, now better known under the initials LSD, but did not discover its mind-altering properties until an accidental ingestion in 1943.

The publicity surrounding the misuse of this synthetic hallucinogen has increased awareness of the historic importance of natural fungal chemicals as part of religious and medicinal ritual. At the forefront of research into the ritual use of fungi were the American R. Gordon Wasson and the Frenchman Roger Heim, while Hofmann and others unravelled the nature of the chemicals involved. (See Heim 1963 and Wasson, Ruck and Hofmann 1978.)

Working in Mexico, Guatamala and surrounding countries they pieced together accounts of the ceremonial use of hallucinogenic fungi with archaeological finds of frescoes depicting fungi and tiny stone statues of human figures with mushroom-like tops (some dating back to 500 BC). Evidence suggests that hallucinogenic fungi were used both in the Mayan and Aztec religions, with species of *Psilocybe* (still found in the localities today) being the most likely fungi involved.

The mind-altering chemicals, psilocybin and

Fig. 28: 'Mushroom Stones' from Guatamala.

psilocin, present in the American species are also found in some British species, most notably *Psilocybe semilanceata* – Liberty Cap or Magic Mushroom (see p. 79). Although this common species has been extensively used 'for pleasure' since the 1960s, there is no evidence of any earlier ritual use.

Of all the fungi found in folklore the most important is the Fly Agaric (*Amanita muscaria* p. 155). Its representation in children's picture books (usually with an assemblage of little folk or witches), on Christmas cards and on a range of ornaments (especially as a resting place for garden gnomes), ensures its high profile as the archetypal toadstool. Even academic books help to substantiate one important myth: that the Fly Agaric is deadly poisonous. In addition to its hallucinogenic properties it does produce symptoms of sickness and diarrhoea but such poisoning is usually mild and there are very few reports of its ingestion leading to a fatality.

Wasson (1967) argued that it is indeed the archetypal toadstool, noting that its older, local name in many parts of Europe is linked to the toad. Since the coming of Christianity the toad has inspired revulsion and fear; possibly because it had been honoured by many pagan sects. Its use in the witches' flying brew (highlighted by Shakespeare's Macbeth) maintained its reputation. The Fly Agaric was also used in flying potions (the Austrian name translates as witch's mushroom) but this is not apparently the link with its English name.

The English 'Fly Agaric' is explained in all fungus books as being so named from its historic use (steeped in water and sugar) as a fly killer in many areas of Europe, and the first written record of this dates from the 13th century. A more intriguing and probably much earlier link is with the fly of madness, or divine possession – associated with its hallucinogenic properties. Terms such as 'a fly in your ear' or 'a bee in your bonnet' are found all over Europe.

The use of *Amanita muscaria* as an inebrient in parts of Siberia has been recorded by visitors from the 17th century onwards. Wasson (1967) concluded that the mushrooms had to be dried first, were often steeped in plant extracts and that the habit of drinking urine from a person who had eaten the mushroom was widespread, with similar effects to that of consuming the fungus. (In some languages the term for getting drunk is literally 'becoming bemushroomed' and the above may account for the strange phrase 'getting pissed'.) Reindeer were also noted for their passion for the mushroom and for human urine!

The great Victorian mycologist Mordecai Cooke included the above information in his *Plain and Easy Account of British Fungi* (1862) in which he also relates that one effect of eating the mushroom is to create delusions as to the size of objects. Charles Dodgson (Lewis Carroll) is known to have read a review of Cooke's book and this may have been the origin of Alice's experience with the mushroom that enabled her to control her height. See Fig. 29.

Wasson argues that the use of Fly Agaric goes back thousands of years but would formerly have been reserved for the shaman or healer who would use the mushroom to enable him to communicate with the spirits and so cure the sick. Taylor (1980) neatly uses this information to explain a more modern myth: Father Christmas clothed in the red and white of the Fly Agaric is shown flying through the air in an intoxicated state, pulled by reindeer that alight on a roof enabling entry down the chimney. The shaman entered the Siberian dwelling via the smoke hole which also served as the entrance, but his gifts were those of healing.

Wasson puts forward *Amanita muscaria* as the divine Soma, central to the ancient Vedic scriptures brought by the Aryan peoples out of Europe into the Indus Valley about 1500 BC and from which Hinduism had its roots. More controversial was Allegro's (1970) allegation (based on his translations of the Dead Sea Scrolls) that Christianity is based on an *Amanita* cult.

Whatever the truth may be, there is sufficient supposition, myth and magic surrounding the Fly Agaric to uphold its place as **the** most fascinating toadstool!

Fig. 29: *"She stretched herself up on tiptoe, and peeped over the edge of the mushroom..."* (Lewis Carroll, 'Alice in Wonderland').

The Healing Power of Fungi

MANY FUNGI PRODUCE CHEMICALS THAT KILL OR ARREST THE GROWTH of other organisms (including other fungi and herbivores), thus reducing competition for food. Where the action takes place against micro-organisms such as bacteria, the chemicals are known as antibiotics. The medical significance of the antibiotic penicillin, produced by the mould *Penicillium notatum* and discovered by Fleming in 1928, lay dormant until the early 1940s when Chain and Florey initiated its development as a pharmaceutical drug.

The success of penicillin in the fight against bacterial infection encouraged research into other species of fungi and other micro-organisms such as the actinomycetes. Species of *Streptomyces* in particular yielded a number of important antibiotics such as streptomycin, which greatly reduced mortality from tuberculosis. In Britain today one in six prescriptions is for an antibiotic, although many are now produced synthetically.

Practitioners of herbal medicine have long used mouldy bread or fruit to treat wounds, implying that penicillin may have been used for thousands of years. Wainwright *et al* (1992) tested the effectiveness of mouldy oranges and found that they did indeed show anti-bacterial activity, although this was due to the fungal toxin patulin rather than the low levels of penicillin.

Herbals mention the use of fungal fruitbodies as styptics (to stop bleeding). These included the Hoof Fungus (*Fomes fomentarius*), a species common on birch in Scotland, less common on beech in eastern and southern England. A bracket fungus not found in Britain (*Lariciformis officinalis*) was described in ancient Greek and Roman herbals as a styptic and for its purgative and antiperspirant properties. The active chemical, agaricic acid, was still being used this century to prevent night sweating in tuberculosis patients.

Puffballs, including species of *Lycoperdon* and *Bovista*, are edible in the immature stage (pp. 70–71) but the mature spore mass was used in Europe as a wound dressing. Other puffball species are still used in a similar way in central India (Rai *et al* 1993) along with other fungi to treat conjunctivitis and increase lactation in nursing mothers. The Chinese pharmacopoeia still makes use of puffball spore dust both to arrest bleeding and to treat throat infections (Keys 1976). European herbals depicted Jew's Ear (*Auricularia auricula-judae* p. 146) as a cure for sore throats. A gargle was prepared from an infusion of the gelatinous fruitbody.

Many medicinal drugs are poisonous in high dose but beneficial in small amounts. This is the case with the alkaloids found in ergot (*Claviceps purpurea*) – mentioned in the preceding section. Long before the discovery of the connection between the fungus and the disease it caused, midwives were using small quantities to ease child birth. Oxytocin has now largely replaced ergometrine, the drug produced from ergot, to ensure expulsion of the afterbirth. Another preparation from ergot, ergotamine, has been used to treat migraine because it reduces peripheral blood flow and prevents pressure in the temple regions.

Homeopathic medicine uses some very dilute fungal extracts. An extract of the Fly Agaric (or Bug Agaric – *Agaricus muscarius* as it was known to Hahnemann, the founder of modern homeopathy), is used to treat psoriasis, chilblains and some nervous disorders.

Recent advances in medicine are finding novel uses for fungal chemicals. Cyclosporin A, discovered in 1976 in a species of *Tolypocladium*, suppresses the body's immune response and is now routinely used to prevent the rejection of transplanted organs. It is proving very successful in the treatment of severe eczema and may yet replace the use of steroids. Gliotoxin, originally isolated from *Aspergillus fumigatus* in 1932, is now being investigated as a cancer-treating agent because of its role in triggering apoptosis or cell suicide.

The Identification of Fungi

AS WITH PLANTS AND ANIMALS, each species of fungus has a set of characteristics which separates it from all other species. These include macroscopic features such as size and colour of the fruitbody, and microscopic features such as spore shape. Whilst the separation of some closely related species requires microscopic examination, the edible species described in this book can all be identified using the naked eye.

When confronted with an unknown fungus beginners tend to observe features such as size, shape and colour of the fruitbody and little else. Unfortunately these three factors are all extremely variable and are rarely sufficient in themselves to ensure accurate identification. The Death Cap, for instance, is normally olive-green but ranges from white through ochre to grey. Identification of fungi requires the use of at least four senses: sight, touch, smell and taste – it is not possible to hear them, but a sixth sense is certainly useful for finding them!

The following features need to be noted for the identification of any unknown fungus. They are listed in the same order as in the species descriptions that follow in the main part of the book. Habitat, substratum and habit of growth must be recorded in the field together with any colour change on handling.

HABITAT

Where is the fungus growing?
For example: grassland (where there are no trees), parkland (grass and trees) or broad-leaved wood land (in this case it is important to identify the closest tree species). Soil type, e.g. sand or chalk, wet or dry, is also important.

SUBSTRATUM

What is the fungus growing on?
For example: soil, moss, dung, leaf litter, living wood (identify tree if possible) or tree stump. Many fungi are associated with tree roots that can extend 50 m from the trunk where the mycorrhizal fungus (see p. 8) may appear in grassland.

HABIT OF GROWTH

How does the fungus grow?
For example: solitary, in a small group, in a ring, tufted (stem bases fusing).

SEASON

When does the fungus grow?
See the section 'When do Fungi Fruit?' (pp. 11–13). In this book we include a histogram on the edible species pages to indicate when they are most likely to be found.

FEATURES OF THE FRUITBODY

The features described in this section apply to the 'Agarics' – mushrooms and toadstools that typically comprise a cap bearing gills or tubes together with a central stem. Descriptions of edible species of bracket fungi, puffballs, morels and truffles will not include all of the following features.

In some species the very **young** fruitbody (hyphal structure that produces and bears spores) is totally enclosed in a sheet-like universal veil. Later this may leave remnants on the cap or at the stem base of the fungus.

1) SIZE – The diameter in centimetres. The normal range, e.g. 4–8 cm, is shown together with the species illustrations.

Size varies with food and water availability, age and genetic make up of an individual; as it does in people. Occasional specimens may be found outside the range but if several are bigger or smaller than the range they probably belong to a different species.

Lookalike species depicted alongside the main edible species in this book are of comparable size unless otherwise stated.

2) SHAPE

a) Convex

b) Flattened

c) Depressed

d) Funnel-shaped (infundibuliform)

e) Bell-shaped (campanulate)

f) Conical

Any of these shown here can also be described as **umbonate** (having a central hump) see above.

3) Margin
This may be continuous with rest of the cap or:

a) turned down

b) inrolled

c) turned up

In addition the margin may be:

d) grooved (sulcate)

e) wavy or split

f) bearing the remains of the partial veil and may be paler or darker than the rest of the cap.

4) Texture

Observe and feel the cap. Is it:
a) smooth and dry – shiny or matt?
b) viscid (wet and slippery to the touch)?
c) glutinous (sticky to the touch)?
d) wrinkled?
e) with the texture of kid leather?
f) with small fibres (fibrils) usually flattened down (adpressed)?

g) with radially arranged fibrils?

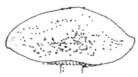

h) with very small particles (mealy)?

i) with scales (squamose)?
j) with dense woolly fibrils (tomentose)?
k) with the remains of the universal veil?
The skin (cuticle) may peel easily or not and may not quite reach the margin. It may crack to reveal the underlying flesh.

5) Colour – is the cap uniform or is the centre darker or lighter?
– is it different in young and old specimens?
– any changes on handling or bruising?

Gills (lamellae) or tubes or spines.

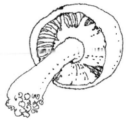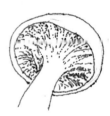

In some species the immature gills or tubes are covered with a protective **partial veil** which is either like a sheet or a cobweb (cortina).

1) Attachment to Stem – best seen by slicing cap and stem in half vertically (see line drawings with illustrations of main species).

a) Free (not attached to stem)

b) Adnexed (attached at top only)

c) Sinuate (notched near the stem giving a moat-like appearance round the stem)

d) Adnate (fully attached)

e) Decurrent (running down the stem)

2) Spacing – extremes are distant (far apart) and crowded.

The presence or absence of **intermediate gills** that do not continue to the stem affects spacing.

3) Width – if especially thick or thin.
Where there are tubes they may be long or short and the openings (pores) small or big (easily visible to the naked eye), round or angular.

4) Texture e.g. brittle, waxy or deliquescent.

5) Colour
This varies with age and may be masked by the spore colour. Gill colour is often different from spore colour. Colour may change on bruising or gills may exude a fluid on cutting.

Spore Print

To determine the size and shape of fungal spores requires the use of a high-power microscope but the colour of a mass of spores can be ascertained from a spore print. This is one of the least variable features and is often an essential piece of identification when trying to separate edible species from their poisonous lookalikes.

Very young and very old specimens will not produce spores so select a 'middle-aged' one, cut off the stem and lay the cap gills-down on a piece of paper, glass or clear plastic. Ideally the paper should be half white and half black as white spores do not show up well on white paper! Cover the cap to maintain the humidity and leave it for at least three hours.

Examine the print under natural light and check it against the colour shown for each edible species. If the other features appear to fit but the spore colour does not you have probably misidentified your find so **do not eat it**.

Stem *(Stipe)*

1) Size – As with the cap, stem measurements are given as a range, the first figure being the length of the stem plus the thickness of the cap, the second being the stem width e.g. 3–6 cm x 6–8 mm (see measurements on cross-section diagrams with main species illustrations).

2) SHAPE

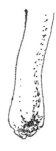

a) Equal (parallel sided)

b) Tapering to a narrow base (in most cases the stem continues into the substratum in a root-like manner)

c) Tapering from a broader base

d) With a bulbous base

e) Emerging from a sack-like **volva** (remains of veil)

In cross section the stem is normally round but it may be flattened or grooved. In some species two or more stems may fuse.

The stem can be solid or hollow.

3) ATTACHMENT TO CAP

a) Central

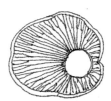

b) Excentric

c) Lateral

4) TEXTURE
See cap features.

5) COLOUR

When the stem has the same colour as the cap it is said to be **concolorous**. Colour and other features may vary from base to apex and above or below a ring, if present.

6) RING (*Annulus*)

Where present this is the remnant on the stem of the partial veil.

The ring may:

a) be half way up the stem, or higher, or lower (see above)

b) hang down/stand up from the stem (see above)

c) be movable up and down the stem

d) appear double (see above)

e) be only transient, as it washes off.

7) FERROUS SULPHATE TEST

A crystal of ferrous sulphate rubbed on the stem of Russula species produces either no response or a variety of colours, including apricot and green, hence separating closely-related species (see pp. 86–87).

Flesh

This refers both to the cap tissue above the gills or tubes and to the stem tissue. In edible species the texture, smell and taste of the flesh are of prime importance.

1) TEXTURE e.g. soft, firm, watery or rubbery. Some species release fluid from the cut flesh (e.g. Milk Caps).

2) COLOUR – this may be different under the skin and in the stem base. Look for changes on cutting or on cooking.

3) SMELL – the overall smell is described in this section.
Smell is the most difficult of the senses to characterise and is usually compared with a well-known scent e.g. 'smells of aniseed' or 'like flour'. Best noted in the field and before mixing with other specimens.

4) TASTE – Tasting does not mean eating; a small piece is chewed for about a minute and then spat out. This test is only done to distinguish between closely related species (usually of the genus *Lactarius* or *Russula*) and must not be carried out on a totally unknown species or on any species of *Amanita*. In some species a strong taste is greatly reduced on cooking.

Key

THIS KEY IS INTENDED TO GUIDE YOU to the appropriate pages of the book, where you can compare your specimen with the descriptions. Remember that this book describes only some of the fungi you may find, so if you are interested in identifying species which are not edible, you will need one of the books recommended on p. 183. At each number in the key you will be offered alternative descriptions: a), b), c), etc. Choose the description that fits your specimen. At the end of that line you will either be offered the name of the fungus or be told which number in the key to go to next. See p. 186 for an explanation of terms.

1 a) shelf- or bracket-shaped with pores below, on wood: Polypores p. 141
  b) cauliflower-shaped, on ground: Cauliflower Fungus p. 174
  c) ear-shaped, on wood: Jew's Ear p. 146
  d) small brown sausage-shaped, in grass, flowers: Ergot p. 75
  e) funnel-shaped, smooth underneath, on ground: Horn of Plenty p. 116
  f) spherical to conical, with or without stalk: go to 2
  g) umbrella-shaped (like a mushroom): go to 5

2 a) with hollow stalk: Morels p. 122
  b) stalk solid or absent: go to 3

3 a) growing below ground: Truffles p. 120
  b) growing on ground or on wood: go to 4

4 a) young flesh white, mature skin thin: Puffballs pp. 68, 125
  b) young flesh dark, mature skin thick: Earthballs p. 162

5 a) cap with spiny pegs underneath: Hedgehog Fungus p. 118
  b) cap with interconnected shallow ridges underneath: Chanterelle p. 114
  c) cap with pores underneath: Boletes pp. 92, 159, 170
  d) cap with gills underneath go to 6

6 a) spore print dark (dark pink, brown or black): go to 7

b) spore print pale (white, cream, yellow, lilac, pale pink): go to 14

7 a) spore print dark pink: go to 8
  b) spore print brown: go to 10
  c) spore print black: go to 13

8 a) gills free from stem: Fawn Mushroom p. 132
  b) gills attached to the stem: go to 9

9 a) gills decurrent, smell of fresh meal: The Miller p. 110
  b) gills sinuate: Livid Entoloma p. 76

10 a) spore print dark brown, gills free: Mushrooms (*Agaricus spp*) pp. 47, 78, 105, 168
  b) spore print purplish-brown, gills attached to stem: go to 11
  c) spore print rusty brown, gills attached to stem: go to 12

11 a) medium-sized, growing in tufts on wood: Sulphur Tuft p. 163
  b) small, growing singly in grassland: Liberty Cap p. 79

12 a) growing in tufts on wood, gills adnexed: Two-toned Pholiota p. 134
  b) growing on the ground, gills deeply decurrent: Brown Roll-rim p. 158

13 a) gills and cap dissolving to black inky liquid: Ink Caps pp. 54, 74

b) gills and cap remaining firm: Weeping Widow p. 56

14 a) cap flesh crumbly (like fresh Lancashire cheese): go to 15
   b) cap flesh firm, does not crumble between the fingers: go to 16

15 a) damaged gills exude white or orange juice: Milk Caps pp. 90, 161, 166
   b) damaged gills do not exude juice: Russulas pp. 84, 178

16 a) gills thick and waxy, always in grassland: Wax Caps p. 61
   b) gills not thick and waxy, in grassland or woods: go to 17

17 a) gills free from stem: go to 18
   b) gills attached to stem: go to 19

18 a) with volva at base of stem: *Amanita spp* p. 151
   b) stem without volva at base: Parasol Mushrooms pp. 58, 81

19 a) gills decurrent (deeply attached): go to 20
   b) gills adnexed, adnate or sinuate (narrowly attached): go to 23

20 a) growing on wood: go to 21
   b) growing on the ground: go to 22

21 a) stem excentric or lateral, without ring: Oyster Mushrooms p. 128
   b) stem central, with ring: Honey Fungus p. 138

22 a) gills forking towards cap margin: False Chanterelle p. 177
   b) each gill separate from the others: *Clitocybe spp* pp. 80, 100

23 a) growing on wood, with velvety stem: Velvet Shank p. 136
   b) growing on the ground, stem smooth: go to 24

24 a) gills distant from each other: go to 25
   b) gills crowded: go to 26

25 a) whitish, in grassland: Fairy-ring Champignon p. 66
   b) brown-pink or purple, in woodland: Deceivers p. 112

26 a) whitish, smell of new meal, in spring: St George's Mushroom p. 52
   b) some part purple-lilac, in autumn or winter: Blewits pp. 64, 102

Edible Species in Grassland

This section includes fungi typically found in permanent grazed pasture, mown lawns, playing fields and roadside verges. Also included are species often found among short heathland vegetation. The most fruitful areas tend to be old, undisturbed grassland fertilised only by animal dung. Newly sown, artificially fertilised grassland is much less productive!

The grassland habitat also occurs in open woodland and especially on woodland ridges. The presence of trees does not prevent the growth of grassland fungi.

Field Mushroom

Agaricus campestris L. ex Fr. *(Psalliota campestris)*

T he most well-known wild species and for many people the only one deemed safe to eat; all others being considered dangerous toadstools. 'Mushrooms are edible and I know a mushroom when I see one' is a common boast, but the fact is that not all the 40-odd British mushroom species are edible, and the problem is knowing which mushroom has been collected. The Yellow-staining Mushroom is easily mistaken for the Field Mushroom and may produce alarming symptoms: for every wild fungus, accurate identification is essential.

EDIBLE
Agaricus campestris

COOKING AND EATING
The most versatile of all edible fungi and small ones can safely be eaten raw (sliced in salads). 'Flats' can be stuffed (include the chopped stem) and baked. They do not have to be peeled. Old specimens are prone to maggots especially in the stem. Not worth freezing or drying; use them fresh.

3-10cm
3-8cm
1-1.5cm

J
F
M
A
M
J 🍄🍄🍄
J 🍄
A 🍄
S 🍄🍄🍄🍄🍄🍄🍄🍄
O 🍄🍄🍄🍄🍄
N 🍄🍄
D

KEY FEATURES: Young specimens have crowded, bright pink gills enclosed in a white veil. At maturity the gills are free and dark chocolate brown (the spore colour), the stem bears a transient membranous ring and the cut white flesh colours faintly pink.

HABITAT: Grass kept short by grazing or mowing including meadows, parks, lawns, golf courses and woodland rides.

FREQUENCY: Common. Locally abundant, sometimes in fairy rings.

SEASON: Early summer to late autumn, especially after rain (see histogram).

CAP: The button stage is white, dry, firm and domed. The margins are covered with remnants of the veil and remain inrolled until maturity when the centre of the now flat cap may break up into small, pale brown scales.

GILLS: At first totally enclosed in a white veil. Crowded and free. Ageing from deep pink through chocolate brown to black when they become soft and wet.

SPORE PRINT: Very dark brown (see picture)

STEM: Short, white, bruises brown. Solid then spongy. Simple, white, thin, transient ring.

FLESH: Soft and white, with slight reddening in cut stem. Smell and taste stronger than most shop mushrooms.

LOOKALIKES

All species of Agaricus have free gills that mature purple-brown, a ring (which may rub off) and a very dark brown spore print. Two species that may occur in the same habitat as the Field Mushroom are:

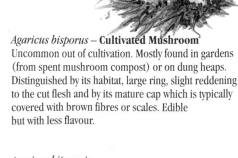

Agaricus arvensis – **Horse Mushroom** (see p. 50)
Distinguished by its larger size (up to twice as big), cap and stem that bruise yellow-brown, grey-coloured young gills, a large, persistent, double ring and flesh smelling of bitter almonds or aniseed. Edible and good.

Two species with slightly different habitats are:

Agaricus xanthodermus –
Yellow-staining Mushroom (see p. 78)
Distinguished by the unpleasant ink-like smell, flattened top of the button stage, white- or grey-coloured young gills, and cut flesh in stem base rapidly yellowing as do cap margin and stem on handling. Poisonous to some, causing sickness and diarrhoea for several days. Occasional, commoner in some years.

Agaricus bisporus – **Cultivated Mushroom**
Uncommon out of cultivation. Mostly found in gardens (from spent mushroom compost) or on dung heaps. Distinguished by its habitat, large ring, slight reddening to the cut flesh and by its mature cap which is typically covered with brown fibres or scales. Edible but with less flavour.

Agaricus bitorquis
Typically found by roads, even coming through pavements from as early as April. Distinguished by its habitat and unusual double ring, the lower one sheath-like. Edible but usually found in polluted habitats.

Early in the season confusion is possible with:

In a separate genus is a fungus very similar to the Field Mushroom:

Calocybe gambosa –
St George's Mushroom (see p. 52)
A similar size and colour, but distinguished by the white sinuate gills and spore print, lack of ring and strong mealy smell. Edible and good. Common in grassland, hedgerows and scrubby woodland from April to July.

Leucoagaricus leucothites
Distinguished by the gill colour which remains white or pale pink and the white spore print. Uncommon in southern England. **Poisonous,** causing gastric upsets.

If the mushrooms are collected in the vicinity of **trees** care must be taken to avoid:

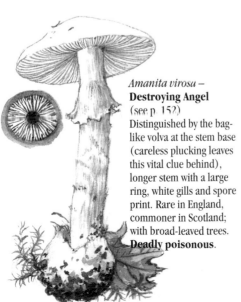

Amanita virosa –
Destroying Angel
(see p. 152)
Distinguished by the bag-like volva at the stem base (careless plucking leaves this vital clue behind), longer stem with a large ring, white gills and spore print. Rare in England, commoner in Scotland; with broad-leaved trees. **Deadly poisonous**.

Inocybe patouillardii –
Red-staining Inocybe (see p. 77)
Distinguished by the more conical cap with wavy, split margins. Cap, stem and olive-yellow gills all bruise red. Cut flesh also reddens. There is no ring, the flesh smells of rotting fruit and the spore print is clay-brown. **Very poisonous.** Among grass in woods and parks, less rare in the south.

Horse Mushroom

Agaricus arvensis Schaeff. ex Secr. *(Psalliota arvensis)*

COOKING AND EATING
The thick flesh and nutty flavour are regarded by some as superior to the Field Mushroom. The large caps are excellent for stuffing. Sadly, Horse Mushrooms are also favoured by maggots so do check as you pick to avoid disappointment.

Not easily overlooked as it often forms very large fairy rings of plate-sized mushrooms. Apart from its size, it differs from the Field Mushroom in its smell and a tendency of the cap and stem to bruise yellow-brown on handling. These features have cast suspicion on the Horse Mushroom's edible qualities and many people spurn it. It is in fact edible and tasty, being frequently sold in greengrocers.

Care must be taken to separate it from species that bruise bright yellow as these include the poisonous Yellow-staining Mushroom.

5-20cm

5-15cm

1.5-2cm

J
F
M
A
M
J 🍄🍄
J 🍄
A 🍄
S 🍄🍄🍄🍄🍄🍄
O 🍄🍄🍄🍄🍄🍄🍄
N 🍄🍄🍄
D

KEY FEATURES: Large white cap becoming ochreous with age and handling. Gills free, grey-white before maturing dark brown (the spore colour). A persistent, large, double ring. Aniseed smell.

HABITAT: Permanent pastures, lawns and occasionally on road verges and disturbed ground. Horses are not essential!

FREQUENCY: Frequent. Gregarious, often in large fairy rings.

SEASON: Early summer to late autumn (see histogram).

CAP: Domed button maturing flat and large. White, becoming ochreous with age and (slowly) on handling. Smooth or with marginal scales and veil remnants.

GILLS: Enclosed in a white veil in the button stage. Crowded, broad, free; grey-white, later dark brown.

SPORE PRINT: Very dark brown (see picture).

STEM: Base swollen, soon hollow, white bruising ochraceous, not yellow if cut. Large, permanent, skirt-like, two-layered ring; the lower part star-shaped.

FLESH: Thick, firm and white; slight browning in stem. Smells of aniseed or bitter almonds when fresh; tastes nutty.

LOOKALIKES

All Agaricus species have free gills and dark brown spores. Two similar sized, species are:

Agaricus xanthodermus –
Yellow-staining Mushroom
(see p. 78)
Distinguished by the unpleasant ink-like smell, flattened top of the button stage and the cut flesh in stem base rapidly yellows as do the cap margin and stem on handling. **Poisonous** to some, causing sickness and diarrhoea for several days. Occasional but often in rings. Grassland and woodland.

Agaricus macrosporus
Very large cap, long remaining convex  white but slowly ageing and bruising ochre. Young gills are pink. Stem stout, with tiny white scales below the large ring. Cut flesh in stem base pinking. Smell mushroomy or slightly of aniseed. In rings, more common in the north. Edible.

A **woodland** species with an aniseed smell and ochre-yellow coloured cap is:

Agaricus silvicola –
The Wood Mushroom (see p. 108)
Distinguished by its woodland habitat, smaller size and less fleshy cap and stem. The cap becomes deep yellow with age. Often with a distinct bulb at the stem base. In broad-leaved and coniferous woodland. Occasional. Edible.

51

St George's Mushroom
Calocybe gambosa (Fr.) Donk. *(Tricholoma gambosum)*

COOKING AND EATING
Can become dry and tough so best collected young and after rain. The mealy smell and taste is much reduced on cooking and its value lies in the firm, dry flesh and the early season which also reduces the chance of maggots. Especially good when grilled or fried with garlic.

An aptly named fungus which appears around about 23 April and reaches its peak in May. With the notable exception of the Morel there are few other edibles this early. Opinion as to its culinary ranking is divided; it is appreciated in France and some other European countries but it is not even mentioned in a recent book on British edibles! Some find the chunky texture and mealy smell to their liking, others do not; it really is a matter of taste. There is one confusable species which fruits early and is deadly poisonous.

J
F
M
A 🍄🍄🍄🍄
M 🍄🍄🍄🍄🍄🍄🍄🍄🍄🍄🍄🍄🍄
J 🍄🍄
J
A
S
O
N
D

5-12cm

4-10cm

2-4cm

KEY FEATURES: Cap, gills and stem all creamy-white. Dry, fleshy cap with wavy edges. Thick ringless stem, sinuate gills and a white spore print. Smells and tastes strongly of meal.
HABITAT: Usually among grass in open pasture, road verges, lawns and sand dunes or in hedgerows and woodland margins with spring flowers. Commoner on calcareous soils.
FREQUENCY: Common, communal, often in rings.
SEASON: April to June (see histogram).
CAP: Fleshy and dense when young. Domed with inrolled edges then flatter but with wavy, sometimes split edges. White, maturing pale tan; dry and smooth.
GILLS: Crowded, as cap colour, sinuate.
SPORE PRINT: White (see picture).
STEM: Broad, solid; often curved and thicker at base, as cap colour.
FLESH: White, firm, 2–3 cm thick. Strong smell and taste of meal when young, less when old and dry.

Inocybe patouillardii –
Red-staining Inocybe (see p. 77)
With a more conical cap, margins often wavy and split.
Older caps bruise brick-red as do the stems, olive-
yellow gills and cut flesh. Clay-brown spore print; flesh
smells of rotting fruit. **Poisonous,** can prove fatal.
Occasional, most frequent in the south among grass in
woods and parks, commoner on calcareous soils and
fruiting as early as May, continuing to late autumn.

Entoloma lividum – **Livid Entoloma** (see p. 76)
Uncommon but forming rings in similar habitats to
Calocybe. It also has a creamy-white large, fleshy cap
with wavy, inrolled edges, sinuate gills, a broad stem and
a mealy smell when young. It is distinguished by the gills
which start pale yellow and mature flesh coloured with a
pink spore print. Older specimens have a rancid smell.
It usually fruits later than *Calocybe*. **Poisonous,**
causing severe gastric upsets.

Clitopilus prunulus – **The Miller** (see p. 110)
Smaller and less fleshy, with a thin stem and strongly
decurrent pink gills and a pink spore print but of
comparable cap colour to *Calocybe* and also smelling
strongly of meal. In open woodland. Edible.

Agaricus campestris –
Field Mushroom (see p. 47)
Distinguished by the dark brown spores which
colour the initially pink gills, and the ring on
the stem. Early fruiters can overlap with
Calocybe. Edible and good.

Shaggy Ink Cap or Lawyer's Wig
Coprinus comatus (Mull.) Pers.

Common in and around towns which, together with its size, gregarious nature and long fruiting season, makes it noticeable. Its edible qualities are underestimated and there is only one species with which it can readily be confused.

COOKING AND EATING
Any soil or leaves sticking to the cap can be removed with a damp cloth. Cook as soon after gathering as possible. Must be eaten young: place cut halves gill down in a small amount of butter, fry quickly on a high heat or deep fry, coated in breadcrumbs. Older ones can be turned into ketchup or cooked slowly, liquidised and added to a stock to make a wonderful (if odd-coloured) soup.

3-7cm

8-25cm

1-1.5cm

J
F
M
A 🍄
M 🍄
J 🍄
J 🍄
A 🍄
S 🍄🍄🍄🍄
O 🍄🍄🍄🍄🍄🍄🍄🍄🍄🍄
N 🍄🍄
D 🍄

KEY FEATURES: Appears stemless when young, cap covered with off-white shaggy scales, older caps dissolving from the base into a black fluid.

HABITAT: Road verges, lawns and playing fields especially after disturbance and on buried rubbish. In grass and other herbaceous vegetation; sometimes under trees.

FREQUENCY: Common, often in very large groups, sometimes with the Common Ink Cap.

SEASON: Spring to early winter (see histogram).

CAP: Young ones are smooth, white and shaped like the end of a finger: no stem is visible. As the stem elongates the cap becomes the shape of a rugby ball, with no gills visible. The outer surface breaks up into overlapping shaggy white to pale brown scales (like a lawyer's wig) except at the very top which is smooth and a dirty brown colour. The base of the cap turns pink and then black, pulling away from the stem and giving the fungus a cylindrical shape. The cap then dissolves from the base upwards into a black ink-like fluid leaving only a tiny flat cap on a long stem.

GILLS: Many, crowded, free and elongated. White, then turning pink and finally black.

SPORE PRINT: Black (see picture).

STEM: Smooth, white, hollow, slightly broader at the base and with a movable ring which may break away or slip down.

FLESH: White (when young) and thin. Mushroomy smell, mild taste and no maggots.

Coprinus atramentarius –
Common Ink Cap (see p. 74)
Usually less tall, more bell-shaped and without the large shaggy scales. Margin smooth and grey, apex with tiny fawn scales. Ill-defined ring zone. In small groups, on wood and in grass from buried debris. **This fungus must not be consumed with alcohol (see p. 20) and is best avoided by all but teetotallers!**

Coprinus picaceus – **Magpie Fungus**
Young white specimens are easily confused with the button stage of *C. comatus* but mature caps are grey-black, covered with small white patches. Stem has no ring. In ones and twos usually in beech woods and not common. Possibly **poisonous** to some people, so avoid.

Other species of *Coprinus*
These are typically much smaller and often grow in specialised habitats such as on tree stumps, bonfire sites and dung. All have black spore prints.

Species of *Psathyrella*
In similar habitats with dark spore colours and brittle stems but with a more expanded cap, not dissolving and with no cap scales or stem ring. Mostly fawn or brown coloured and not worth eating.

Weeping Widow

Lacrymaria lacrymabunda (Bull.ex.Fr.) Pat. *(Lacrymaria velutina)*
(Psathyrella lacrymabunda) (Psathyrella velutina)

COOKING AND EATING
Discard the stems and fry the caps whole in hot butter or deep fry in batter. Do not overcook. Serve with sweet pickle to counteract the slightly bitter taste or mix with Shaggy Inkcap. Rarely causes mild digestive upset.

D espite the name it is not a widow maker – the weeping refers to the drops of moisture on the gills; the widow to the black veil round the edge of the cap. Many books pass it over because of its slightly bitter taste but it is easily identified and we find it complements species such as the Shaggy Inkcap with which it often grows.

3-8cm

6-12cm

0.5-1cm

J
F
M
A
M
J 👤
J 👤
A 👤👤👤
S 👤👤👤👤👤
O 👤👤👤👤👤👤👤👤
N 👤
D

KEY FEATURES: Fibrillose ochre cap with veil remnants at the margin. Brown, mottled gills 'weeping' when moist, with a cobweb-like veil when young. Black spore deposit showing as a ring on the thin, fragile, fibrillose stem.

HABITAT: In grass, herbs and bare soil in pastures, lawns, verges and woodland paths.

FREQUENCY: Common, either solitary or tufted.

SEASON: Summer to the frosts (see histogram).

CAP: Bell shaped, becoming flatter with a broad umbo and an inrolled margin fringed with veil remnants, blackened by the spores. Ochre to clay brown cap streaked with fibres, maturing smooth.

GILLS: Cobweb-like veil protects young brown gills which become mottled and finally black (as the spores mature) but retain a white edge. Gills adnate, crowded and in moist conditions exude tiny dew-like droplets, especially near the stem.

SPORE PRINT: Black (see picture).

STEM: Thin, equal, fragile, paler than the cap. Fibrillose and with a ring zone which blackens with the spores.

FLESH: Tan coloured with a slightly bitter taste.

LOOKALIKES

Psathyrella candolleana
Slightly smaller and less robust but also tufted, with black spores and a fringed cap margin. Distinguished by its paler smooth cap, slim white stem and the absence of gill mottling or weeping. In woods and gardens, usually on or near stumps. Edible but not worthwhile.

Coprinus atramentarius –
Common Ink Cap (see p. 74)
Separated by its greyer colour, deep bell-shaped cap, elongated, non-mottled gills which autodigest into a black fluid on maturity and the smooth white stem. Causes **acute digestive upset** if consumed with alcohol.

Agrocybe praecox
Found in similar habitats and of similar size and appearance, but with a pale tan cap, brown gills (and spore print) and a membranous ring on the smooth stem. Edible but not worthwhile.

Species of mushroom (*Agaricus* see p. 47) often grow in the same habitats but are distinguished by their stouter build, more solid veil, free gills and a ring. Most are edible but see *A. xanthodermus* (p. 78).

N.B. Many species of *Inocybe* have a brown, fibrillose, umbonate cap but are mostly much smaller and they have a clay-brown spore print. Some are **very poisonous** (not illustrated).

Parasol Mushroom

Macrolepiota procera (Scop. ex Fr.) Sing. *(Lepiota procera)*
(Leucocoprinus procerus)

Rivalling the Horse Mushroom in the size of its expanded cap and with a dry texture and excellent flavour, this impressive fungus is a great favourite among mushroom eaters. While its size distinguishes it from the many small *Lepiota* species, some of which are very poisonous, there are a number of similar related species (including the Shaggy Parasol) which cause digestive upsets in some people. In addition some non-related lookalikes are mildly poisonous.

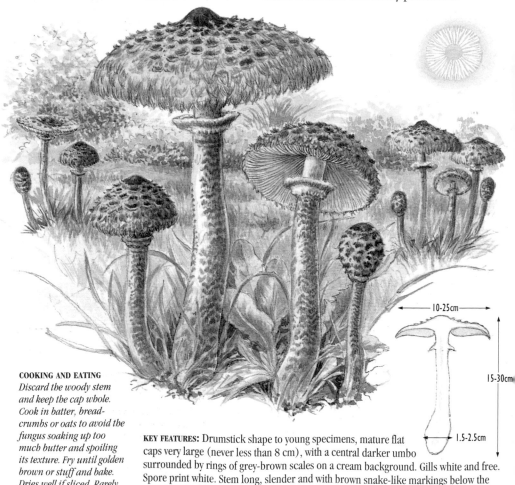

COOKING AND EATING
Discard the woody stem and keep the cap whole. Cook in batter, breadcrumbs or oats to avoid the fungus soaking up too much butter and spoiling its texture. Fry until golden brown or stuff and bake. Dries well if sliced. Rarely maggot infested but older caps may contain tiny mites. Will keep for several days in a refrigerator.

KEY FEATURES: Drumstick shape to young specimens, mature flat caps very large (never less than 8 cm), with a central darker umbo surrounded by rings of grey-brown scales on a cream background. Gills white and free. Spore print white. Stem long, slender and with brown snake-like markings below the movable, double ring.

HABITAT: Among grass in pastures, parks, open woodland, hedges and road verges. Preferring acid soils.

FREQUENCY: Occasional. In small groups or fairy rings. Locally frequent in wet summers.

SEASON: Mid summer to autumn (see histogram).
CAP: Egg shaped; expanding to bell-like and finally very large, dry and flat except for a central brown umbo which is surrounded by concentric pale brown scales on a cream background. The down-turned edge is fringed with veil remnants.
GILLS: Covered by a thick white veil in young specimens. White, crowded, dry and free.
SPORE PRINT: White (see picture).
STEM: Long, slender, tapering from a swollen base. Fibrous but hollow and easily broken. White, covered with snake-like brown markings below the large, double-edged white ring which can be moved on the stem.
FLESH: Thin (the gills are much deeper), white (not reddening on cutting), soft and with a slight earthy smell. Taste sweet and nutty.

J
F
M
A
M
J
J
A 🍄🍄
S 🍄🍄🍄
O 🍄🍄🍄🍄🍄🍄🍄🍄🍄🍄🍄🍄🍄
N 🍄
D

Macrolepiota rhacodes (Lepiota rhacodes) – Shaggy Parasol Mushroom

Cap slightly smaller, but fleshier and with a less pronounced umbo. The smooth brown apex is surrounded by large, pale beige, reflexed fibrous scales. The pale flesh is visible between the shaggy scales. Gills cream, bruising red-brown. Spore print as *procera*. Stem stockier, smooth, white, and lacks the snake-like markings but ages and bruises red-brown. Ring as *procera*. Flesh turning orange-red when cut, especially in stem. Smell stronger than *procera*, slightly sweet.

More common than *procera* in early autumn in woods (especially coniferous) and on compost. Some books recommend this as a highly edible species, as it is to most people but it can cause digestive upsets and skin rashes so **treat with caution**.

12-18cm

12 cm

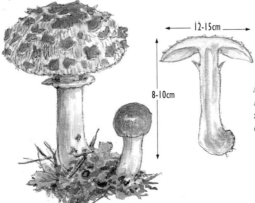

12-15cm

8-10cm

Macrolepiota rhacodes var hortensis
A variety of the above but stockier and with more angular, chestnut-coloured scales. In gardens on compost or rich soil. Edibility as above so **be careful**.

Two edible species similar to *procera* but smaller (cap to 12 cm) are:

Macrolepiota gracilenta – **Slender Parasol**
With a smaller cap bearing less distinct scales which do not reach to the margin and a slimmer, similarly marked, stem. Quite common in grassy places.

Macrolepiota konradii
With a large, brown, smooth central cap area not reaching the margin, less distinctive stem markings and a slight reddening of the flesh.

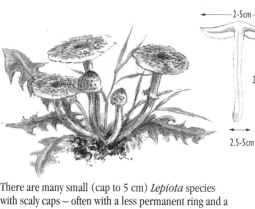

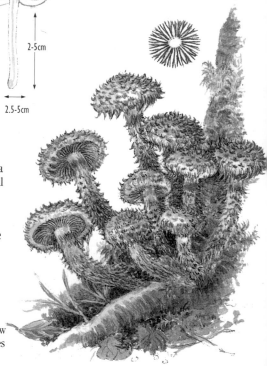

There are many small (cap to 5 cm) *Lepiota* species with scaly caps – often with a less permanent ring and a fruity smell. Some are **deadly poisonous** and all small Parasol lookalikes must be avoided (see p. 81).

All the above species have free gills and white spores which distinguishes them from:

Pholiota squarrosa – **Shaggy Pholiota**
A medium-sized species forming tufts on dead wood near the base of living broad-leaved trees. The orange-brown cap is covered with pointed scales which also cover the stem, below the simple ring. The adnate yellow gills become rusty-brown as the similar coloured spores mature. The bitter flesh causes **digestive upsets**.

Meadow Waxcap

Hygrocybe pratensis (Pers. ex. Fr.) Orton & Watling *(Camarophyllus pratensis) (Hygrophorus pratensis) (Cuphophyllus pratensis)*

EDIBLE
Hygrocybe pratensis

This grassland species is not well known as an edible, possibly because it is more common on upland grssland in the north, but we consider it worthwhile not least because it is not easily confused with any poisonous species. It is often found growing with other waxcaps, many of which are very brightly coloured but not toxic.

COOKING AND EATING
Requires slow cooking to soften the thick flesh and also to reduce the liquid given off; this makes it possible to fry them without any butter or oil! Add garlic or spices to enrich the mild taste. Very good served with puffball, as the different textures and flavours complement each other.

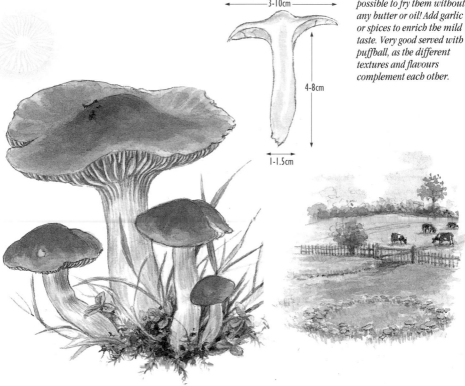

3-10cm

4-8cm

1-1.5cm

KEY FEATURES: Thick, distant, decurrent, waxy, occasionally branching, buff-coloured gills. Cap shape and colour very varied, but typically apricot coloured. Stem merging with the cap and narrowing towards the base. White spore print.

HABITAT: Grazed pastures, lawns and woodland clearings.

FREQUENCY: Very common. Often in rings.

SEASON: Autumn to early winter (see histogram).

CAP: Convex, then flattened or even concave but usually umbonate and with an acute margin; dry, often irregular and cracking. Pale to deep apricot.

GILLS: Colour as cap, thick, distant, very decurrent, waxy and occasionally branching with cross veins visible as wrinkles between the gills.

SPORE PRINT: White (see picture).

STEM: Short, stout, paler than the cap, smooth and narrowing towards the base.

FLESH: Thick at the cap centre, straw yellow, moist. Mild mushroomy smell and taste.

J
F
M
A
M
J
J
A 🍄
S 🍄🍄🍄🍄🍄🍄🍄
O 🍄🍄🍄🍄🍄🍄🍄🍄
N 🍄
D 🍄

Cantharellus cibarius –
Chanterelle (see p. 114)
Similar in size, shape and spore
colour but with a fruity smell and a
yellower colour. Deep wrinkles
replace the gills. Found in moss under
trees. Edible and excellent.

Hygrophoropsis aurantiaca –
False Chanterelle (see p. 177)
More orange-red in colour and thin fleshed with
crowded, non-waxy gills and a narrow stem. White
spore print. Sometimes found in acid grassland.
Poisonous to a minority, not worthwhile to others.

There are a number of other waxcaps with a similar
colour, size and habitat but none are as fleshy, or
have the combination of deeply decurrent gills and a
broad stem. They are mostly not worth eating (e.g.
Hygrocybe quieta, H. lepida, H. reidii).

Other waxcaps that are edible include:

Hygrocybe coccinea – **Scarlet Hood**
One of the commonest of the red waxcaps to be found
from late summer to autumn. Small, smooth, dry,
orange-red cap, concolorous narrow stem and orange,
adnate gills. Other red waxcap species are less good to
eat but are not poisonous.

Hygrocybe nivea (*Camarophyllus niveus*) – **Snowy Waxcap**
A much less fleshy, more greasy, pure white species with a transparent (sometimes upturned) margin to the flat-topped cap and decurrent, white, distant gills. Summer to the frosts. Edible.

A closely related species (*H. virginea*) is more robust and is frequently pink-spotted from a mould infection. Both lack a distinctive smell and often grow with *pratensis* and *coccinea*.

H. nivea and H. virginea can easily be confused with poisonous species that grow in the same habitat including:

Clitocybe dealbata – **Ivory Clitocybe** and the similar *Clitocybe rivulosa* (see p. 80)
Similar in colour, size, shape and spore colour to Snowy Waxcap but the decurrent gills are crowded and non-waxy. *Rivulosa* has a sweet smell, *dealbata* a mealy one. They both contain muscarine and **can be fatal**.

Given the above we **strongly advise against eating white waxcaps;** stick to the orange or red ones!

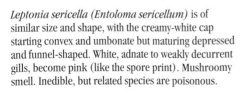
Leptonia sericella (*Entoloma sericellum*) is of similar size and shape, with the creamy-white cap starting convex and umbonate but maturing depressed and funnel-shaped. White, adnate to weakly decurrent gills, become pink (like the spore print). Mushroomy smell. Inedible, but related species are poisonous.

Field Blewit or *Blue Leg*

Lepista saeva (Fr.) Ort. *(Lepista personata)*
(Tricholoma personatum) (Rhodopaxillus saevus)

COOKING AND EATING
The thick stem and fleshy cap are excellent; frying in butter is sufficient. Can be dried (cut into pieces), pickled or frozen (best lightly cooked first).

An excellent edible species, closely related to the Wood Blewit (see p. 102) with which it is sometimes confused. Among grassland species it is comparable with St George's Mushroom (see p. 52) but its lilac-streaked stem is very distinctive. Its strong flavour and thick flesh make it a firm favourite as an edible species.

5-12cm

4-10cm

1.5-2.5cm

J
F
M
A
M
J
J
A
S 🍄🍄🍄🍄🍄🍄🍄
O 🍄🍄🍄🍄
N 🍄🍄🍄🍄🍄🍄🍄
D

KEY FEATURES: Medium sized, thick, pale grey-brown cap with incurved, wavy margins. Crowded, dirty-white sinuate gills and a pale pink spore print. Stocky stem with bright lilac streaks.

HABITAT: Pastures and woodland margins.

FREQUENCY: Occasional, sometimes in fairy rings.

SEASON: Autumn to early winter (see histogram).

CAP: Convex, expanding to flat or depressed, grey-buff, fleshy, smooth and dry with wavy margins, incurved when young.

GILLS: Sinuate, crowded, off-white to flesh-coloured. Easily separated from the flesh.

SPORE PRINT: Pale pink (see picture).

STEM: Short, thick, often swollen at the base. Lilac longitudinal fibres (especially at the base) on a pale background.

FLESH: Thick, firm and white. Smell mealy but sometimes less pleasant. Taste mushroom-like but with a nutty flavour.

LOOKALIKES

In **grassland** the only comparable species are:

Calocybe gambosa – **St George's Mushroom**
(see p. 52)
Can be distinguished by its spring fruiting season,
white stem and spore print but of similar size and shape
to Field Blewit with wavy edges to the cap, sinuate,
crowded gills and a smell of meal. Edible and excellent.

Entoloma lividum – **Livid Entoloma** (see p. 76)
Tan, fleshy cap with wavy margins, inrolled when
young, sinuate gills, pink spores and a mealy smell.
Distinguished by the yellow gills which mature to be
flesh-coloured and lack of lilac on the stem.
Poisonous, causes severe gastric upset.

In **woods** and **parkland** Field Blewit may be mistaken for:

Clitocybe nebularis –
The Clouded Agaric
Also has pale pink spores
and often grows in rings.
Distinguished by its larger
size, grey-coloured cap
and stem, and shortly
decurrent white gills.
Must be well cooked
and can cause gastric
upset, so **avoid**.

Lepista nuda – **Wood Blewit** (see p. 102)
Very similar but with lilac-coloured gills. Edible and
good when well cooked.

Several *Cortinarius* species have purple stems but
these have a cobweb-like veil protecting the young
gills and a rusty-brown spore print. Some species are
very poisonous.

65

Fairy Ring Champignon
Marasmius oreades (Bolt. ex Fr.) Fr.

COOKING AND EATING
Especially good in soups and stews, being used more for its flavour than its bulk. Also very good in an omelette. As with many fungi the flavour is improved with drying – discard the tough stems and thread the caps with cotton. The caps readily reconstitute in water (as they do in the field after rain).

Although many species fruit in rings this is the most well-known not least because its presence in short grass, even when not fruiting, is betrayed by the near circular strips of dying grass encompassed by a ring of dark green grass (see p. 32). Though small, it can be gathered in large numbers, is easily dried and has an excellent flavour. Unfortunately several lookalikes also grow in rings and some are deadly poisonous so check all collected specimens with **great care**.

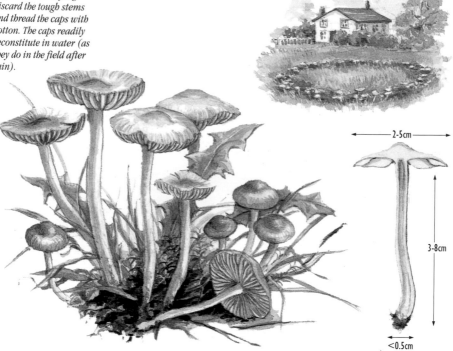

2-5cm

3-8cm

<0.5cm

J
F
M
A 🍄
M 🍄🍄
J 🍄🍄🍄
J 🍄
A 🍄🍄🍄🍄
S 🍄🍄🍄🍄🍄
O 🍄🍄🍄🍄🍄
N 🍄
D

KEY FEATURES: Small, smooth, tan coloured cap and stem. Cap bell-shaped then flat but umbonate. Gills dirty white, adnexed and distant but with intermediate short gills near the margin. White spore print. Stem slender but very pliable.

HABITAT: Short grassland, especially in lawns and parks.

FREQUENCY: Common, more so in wet summers; often in complete or part rings.

SEASON: Early summer to the frosts (see histogram).

CAP: Small, bell-shaped then flatter and umbonate. Smooth but often grooved near the lobed margins. Tan, drying paler.

GILLS: Creamy-white, distant and adnexed but with many shorter intermediate gills which do not reach the stem.

SPORE PRINT: White (see picture).

STEM: Straw-like in colour and diameter, hollow but tough and pliable.

FLESH: White; smells of sawdust or mown grass, nutty sweet taste.

LOOKALIKES

Often growing in rings and sometimes with *Marasmius* are two creamy-brown coloured, similar sized, **deadly poisonous**, white-spored species:

Clitocybe dealbata – **Ivory Clitocybe** (see p. 80)
Cap convex to flat and becoming depressed, lacking marginal grooves but with an incurled edge. Crowded, slightly decurrent gills and a non-pliable stem. Flesh smells mealy.

Clitocybe rivulosa (see p. 80)
As *dealbata* but the cap surface cracks to reveal the flesh which has a slightly sweet smell.

Another lookalike is best recognised by its spore colour:

Nolanea sericea – **Silky Nolanea**
Bell-shaped then flattening but with a central umbo. Dark brown and grooved at the margin when wet but drying paler with a silky gloss. Gills adnexed, grey but later colouring with the pink spores. Flesh smells and tastes of meal. Inedible but some similar, **related species are poisonous**.

The other lookalike occasionally found outside woodland is:

Collybia dryophila – **Russet Tough-shank**
Cap uniform tan, flat and thin. Crowded white gills (and spores). Tough, yellow-brown stem which broadens and darkens at the base. Edible when cooked but not worthwhile.

Giant Puffball

Langermannia gigantea (Batsch ex. Pers.) Rostkov
(*Lycoperdon giganteum*) (*Calvatia gigantea*)

I first found this spectacular fungus over twenty years ago and having quickly ascertained what it was, invited a group of students to share the feast. This was my initiation into the world of fungi and their culinary delights and I still experience a special thrill when I come across one. On one occasion I stalked a white plastic football but this is the only source of confusion with the fully grown fungus. In addition to setting size records the mature puffball was extensively used to staunch blood flow, as tinder and to smoke bees from their honey.

J
F
M
A
M
J
J
A
S
O
N
D

KEY FEATURES: Large size, rounded shape, thin, smooth white skin maturing tan, olive and finally brown. No stalk. Flesh when young like marshmallow but maturing to a brown cotton wool-like mass containing the spores.

HABITAT: Among grass and herbs in pastures, hedgerows, woodlands and gardens especially on fertile soil associated with compost or buried rubbish. Often found amongst nettles.

FREQUENCY: Occasional but recurring on the same site. In small groups, sometimes in rings.

SEASON: Early summer to early autumn, the mature fruitbody persisting (see histogram).

FRUITBODY: Ball or pumpkin shaped, often irregular. Creased at its base where it is attached to the soil by white strands. Skin is smooth and dry, like kid leather, remaining creamy-white as it enlarges but finally darkening through olive to brown when it splits open like a torn paper bag. Internally white and firm, becoming marshmallow-like and then turning bright yellow, olive and finally brown with a mixture of cottony fibres and millions of powdery spores. May take a week to attain full size. White flesh has a mushroomy smell and taste.

SPORE PRINT: Brown.

15-75cm

10-50cm

EDIBILITY

The fruitbody must be immature, with white flesh. It does not require peeling and one specimen can provide several kilos of food. Millipedes and woodlice may excavate parts of the surface layers but they are easily shaken out. The easiest recipe is to cut into 2 cm slices and fry in butter (better still, coat in oats or bread crumbs) until golden brown. It can also be stuffed and baked whole, if the oven is large enough! The overall result is likened to eating hot, mushroom-flavoured marshmallow. A minority find it too rich so do not eat large quantities at the first tasting. It does not dry well and though lightly cooked slices will freeze, they lose their firm texture.

LOOKALIKES

More likely, at a distance, to be taken for a white rabbit or even a lamb but the only possible fungal confusion is:

Calvatia utriformis (Bull. ex. Pers.) Jaap
Commoner in the north in upland pastures and sandy grassland. Reaching the size of a young giant puffball it can easily be distinguished by the flattened top, sterile base (where no spores are present) and the two-layered skin, the outer one cracking into pyramid-shaped warts which detach leaving a honeycomb mosaic on the inner skin. This becomes brown and parchment-like, disintegrating from the apex to reveal the brown spore mass. The non-fertile saucer-like base persists. An autumn species fruiting later than *Langermannia*. When the fertile flesh is still white it is edible and good.

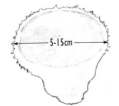

5-15cm

Species found in pastures, lawns, dunes, heaths and moors as distinct from those in woodlands (see p. 125–127):

J
F
M
A
M
J 🍄🍄🍄🍄🍄🍄
J 🍄🍄
A 🍄🍄🍄🍄
S 🍄🍄🍄
O 🍄🍄🍄🍄🍄🍄
N
D

Bovista plumbea

When young it looks like a small golf ball. Flesh firm and white. As the fruitbody matures, the white outer skin splits, falls off and exposes the thin, lead-grey parchment-like inner skin. This darkens with age and finally peels open at the top revealing the red-brown 'cotton wool' spore mass which fills the entire fruitbody at maturity. Often breaking free from the ground and rolling around, releasing brown spores. Appears in late summer to autumn, persisting for many months (see histogram). Common in short lowland grassland (including golf courses), gregarious. Edible when white inside but may need peeling.

J
F
M
A
M
J
J
A 🍄🍄
S 🍄🍄🍄🍄🍄🍄🍄🍄🍄🍄🍄🍄
O 🍄🍄
N 🍄🍄🍄
D

Bovista nigrescens

Very similar to the above but the size of a large golf ball and maturing a shiny, purple-black. More common in upland pasture in the north. Found in the autumn (see histogram). Edibility as above. Both are separated from *Lycoperdon* and *Vascellum* by the lack of a non-fertile stalk region. Often confused with the non-edible golf ball!

J
F
M
A
M
J
J
A 🍄
S 🍄🍄🍄🍄🍄🍄🍄🍄🍄🍄
O 🍄🍄🍄🍄🍄🍄🍄🍄
N 🍄
D

Vascellum pratense

Externally like *Bovista* but flattened and tapering to a stalk region. Covered with small white spines and granules which wash off, leaving a smooth white skin maturing yellow and then pale brown. Spores released through a round apical pore. In cross section the non-fertile stalk area is clearly separated by a membrane. Found summer to autumn (see histogram). Common. Edible when firm and white inside.

Lycoperdon foetidum – **Stinking Puffball**

Most *Lycoperdon* species are woodland dwellers as is this one, but it is also common on heaths and moors. Spherical, with a small stalk-like base. Initially covered with clusters of short brown spines, joined at the top like wigwam poles; these rub off leaving a reticulate pattern on a brown background. Apical, mouth-like opening reveals the olive brown spore mass. Found from summer to autumn (see histogram). Mild-tasting and edible when young, but the unpleasant smell is off-putting ('lycoperdon' means wolf's fart!).

J
F
M
A
M
J
J
A 🍄🍄
S 🍄🍄🍄🍄🍄🍄🍄
O 🍄🍄🍄🍄🍄🍄🍄🍄🍄🍄
N 🍄
D

Calvatia excipuliformis

Grows in parkland, heaths and woodland. Occasional. Larger and with the stalk region comprising up to 75% of the fruitbody, giving it a pestle shape. Initially white and covered with tiny spines and granules, it later becomes smooth, the ochre skin splitting at the apex allowing the spores to escape. Finally the upper fertile region disintegrates leaving the persistent stalk. Found from late summer to autumn (see histogram). Edible and substantial when the flesh is white.

J
F
M
A
M
J
J
A 🍄
S 🍄🍄🍄🍄🍄🍄🍄🍄
O 🍄🍄🍄🍄🍄🍄
N 🍄🍄🍄🍄
D

LOOKALIKES

Very young Mushrooms (*Agaricus spp* – see pp. 47–51) are puffball-shaped but on cutting show a central stem and immature gills. Note that some mushrooms are poisonous.

Found near trees on heaths and moors:

Scleroderma citrinum –
Common Earthball (see p. 162)
Spherical, slightly flattened, almost stalkless. Distinguished from the puffballs by its tough thick, yellow-brown, reptile-like skin and a spore mass which starts whitish but soon becomes purple-black, long remaining firm and with a rubbery smell. Spores released through irregular apical splits. From late summer, persisting into winter. **Vomiting** and **diarrhoea** may occur within 4 hours of ingestion.

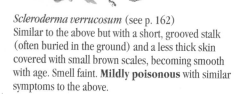

Scleroderma verrucosum (see p. 162)
Similar to the above but with a short, grooved stalk (often buried in the ground) and a less thick skin covered with small brown scales, becoming smooth with age. Smell faint. **Mildly poisonous** with similar symptoms to the above.

When even single trees are present (e.g. in parkland):
Lycoperdon pyriforme – **Stump Puffball**
Grows on wood. This and other woodland species of Puffball (*Lycoperdon spp* – see p. 71) are also edible when eaten young.

Poisonous Species in Grassland

Common Ink Cap
Coprinus atramentarius (Bull.) Fr.

Less conspicuous than the Shaggy Ink Cap (see p. 54) with which it sometimes grows, but equally common and found in a range of habitats including many urban sites. Edible but producing **alarming symptoms** if consumed with alcohol. Only consider its culinary properties if you are teetotal.

2-6cm

5-15cm

1-1.5cm

TOXICITY
Poisonous if consumed within 48 hours of drinking alcohol.
Symptoms can appear soon after the chemical coprine (see p. 20) from the fungus mixes with alcohol in the bloodstream, and include vomiting, diarrhoea, palpitations and a metallic taste. Can be severe enough to result in hospitalisation but fortunately there are no long-term effects. The experience is comparable to that of the drug 'antabuse' used in the treatment of alcoholics, but this has a slightly different chemical structure.

HABITAT: A terrestial species that is associated with buried, rotting wood. It grows close to tree stumps in woodlands but is equally common in gardens and playing fields and is even found emerging through pavements – wherever wood is present underground.
FREQUENCY: Common, usually in groups.
SEASON: Spring to early winter.
CAP: Starting egg-shaped and becoming bell-like as the spores mature. Grey to dirty fawn, shiny, grooved and with small brown scales near the top. May be lobed or split at the margin. Autodigesting to a black inky fluid until very little of the cap remains.
GILLS: Many, crowded and free. Changing from white through grey to black as the spores develop; finally liquifying.
SPORE PRINT: Black (see picture).
STEM: Smooth, white and hollow. Slightly broader at the base just above which an ill-defined ring zone may be present.
FLESH: Thin, white and mushroom scented.

Ergot

Claviceps purpurea (Fr.) Tul.

While poisonings from this fungus are now very rare it is known to have caused suffering and death, especially in France and central Europe, over many years; the earliest record being from the 9th century. It is parasitic on members of the grass family including cereals – rye being the most susceptible. A fuller account of the history and medicinal uses of ergot appears on p. 33 and p. 36. The major problem today is the poisoning of grazing animals which consume infected grass.

HABITAT: Restricted to the flower heads of cereals and grasses – especially rye grass (*Lolium sp.*) and cocksfoot (*Dactylis glomerata*).

FREQUENCY: Common on grasses, rare on cereals due to fungicide sprays.

SEASON: The sclerotia (see below) are found from summer to autumn

SCLEROTIUM AND FRUITBODY: Produces a sclerotium which is like a tiny, hard, curved dark brown to purple-black banana emerging from the flower head as if an overgrown seed. The size varies with the host but is typically 3–10 mm long and 1 mm wide. This sclerotium stage falls to the ground in the autumn and overwinters. In the late spring it produces the fruitbodies – like tiny purple-pink drumsticks, the spores from which infect grass flowers. The fungal tissue invades the ovary and, using nutrients that would have swollen the seed, produces the sclerotium stage.

TOXICITY

The sclerotium contains at least 12 alkaloids (based on lysergic acid), histamine and ergosterol. The toxic effect of a number of these chemicals is manifest after eating bread baked with flour made from ergot-infected grain. Symptoms include severe itching, a burning sensation, gangrene, hallucinations and blindness. Animals that eat infected foodstuffs may develop diarrhoea and foot rot; breeding animals can abort the foetus.

75

Livid Entoloma

Entoloma lividum (Bull.) Quel.
(Entoloma sinuatum) (Rhodophyllus lividus)

TOXICITY
Rarely fatal but it causes severe gastric upset with sickness and stomach cramp and, more seriously, can cause lasting liver damage.

Although this is an uncommon species it has been eaten, with unfortunate consequences, having been confused with St George's Mushroom (p. 52), The Miller (p. 110), Field Blewit (p. 64) and even the Field Mushroom (p. 47). In France it is the cause of 80% of poisonings by fungi.

HABITAT: At field edges and woodland margins. Also on woodland paths and in open broad-leaved woods; usually on rich soil.
FREQUENCY: Uncommon; more frequent in the south.
SEASON: Summer to autumn.
CAP: Large, fleshy, broadly umbonate, irregularly wavy and with an inrolled edge when young. Dry, smooth and initially with a matt surface; later shiny. Colour varies from ivory through dirty yellow (livid) to grey-brown; there are often darker patches.

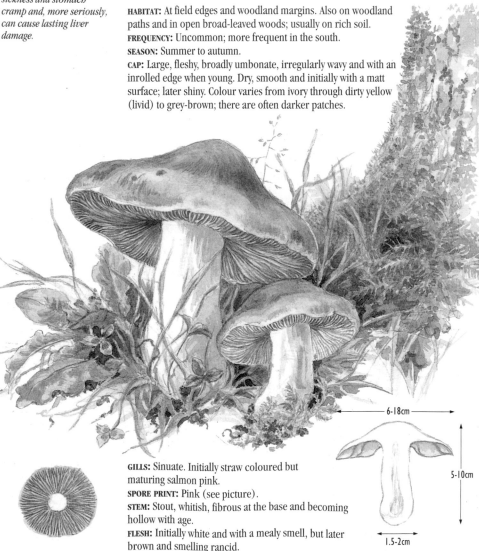

6-18cm

5-10cm

1.5-2cm

GILLS: Sinuate. Initially straw coloured but maturing salmon pink.
SPORE PRINT: Pink (see picture).
STEM: Stout, whitish, fibrous at the base and becoming hollow with age.
FLESH: Initially white and with a mealy smell, but later brown and smelling rancid.

Red-staining Inocybe

Inocybe patouillardii Bres.

There are about 100 species of Inocybe in this country and many are known to contain the poison muscarine, first identified in the Fly Agaric (see p. 155). Most are small and unlikely to be confused with any edible species, although one might be taken for a small Wood Blewit (see p. 102), but the larger Red-staining Inocybe has caused fatalities having been mistaken for Field Mushroom (p. 47) and St George's Mushroom (p. 52).

3-8cm

3-10cm

1-1.5cm

TOXICITY
Said to contain at least 100 times as much muscarine as Fly Agaric. Symptoms occur within 45 minutes of ingestion and include sweating, weeping, slowing of the heart rate and difficulty in breathing. Death is caused by heart failure or asphyxiation. Atropine (from Deadly Nightshade) reverses the symptoms and is used (under medical supervision) as a palliative.

HABITAT: Among grass on woodland rides and margins and in parkland, especially with beech on chalk soils.

FREQUENCY: Uncommon but more frequent in the south.

SEASON: Late spring to autumn.

CAP: Globular when very young (when most like a small Field Mushroom) but becoming bell-shaped and finally flattened with a broad central umbo. Fleshy and silky to the touch. Margin lobed and frequently split. Colour varies from ivory to straw and on bruising, or with age, it turns brick-red on the radiating fibrils.

GILLS: Adnexed, crowded, changing from pale pink through olive-yellow to brick-red; the latter produced on handling.

SPORE PRINT: Dirty brown (see picture).

STEM: Equal or with a bulbous base, stout, solid and often curved. White with brick-red fibrils.

FLESH: Firm and white but slowly reddening when cut. Faint fruity smell, becoming strong and foetid in old specimens.

Yellow-staining Mushroom

Agaricus xanthodermus Genevier *(Psalliota xanthoderma)*

TOXICITY

Common symptoms include stomach ache, sickness and diarrhoea, commencing within two hours of ingestion and lasting for up to 48 hours but with no serious or long-term effects. Occasionally symptoms are more serious, including respiratory problems and even coma.

Uncommon but when found very easily mistaken for a Field (p. 47), Horse (p. 50) or Wood Mushroom (p. 108). Some people can eat it without any ill effects but others suffer from a digestive upset which, while rarely serious, is very unpleasant. This provides an important exception to the popular belief that all Mushrooms are edible.

5-11cm

5-12cm

1-2cm

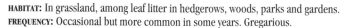

HABITAT: In grassland, among leaf litter in hedgerows, woods, parks and gardens.

FREQUENCY: Occasional but more common in some years. Gregarious.

SEASON: Summer to autumn.

CAP: Flat top of the button stage which then expands and flattens. Creamy-white, often with tiny grey-brown scales at the centre. The skin near the margin turns bright yellow on bruising or scratching.

GILLS: Initially white and enclosed by a veil, they become pale grey-pink, finally maturing to a dark brown. Crowded, free.

SPORE PRINT: Very dark brown (see picture).

STEM: White, swollen at the base and with a large, down-turned ring.

FLESH: White but changing to chrome yellow in the cut stem base.

Smell variously described as of ink, creosote, carbolic and even mouse urine!

Liberty Cap or Magic Mushroom
Psilocybe semilanceata (Fr.) Kummer

Whilst in both North and South America there is a long history of the ritual ingestion of various species of *Psilocybe*, in Britain the eating of *P. semilanceata* for its hallucinogenic effects dates from the 1960s (p. 34). The tiny fungus contains an ester of psilocin (p. 20) which is a controlled drug under the Misuse of Drugs Act and any preparation of the fungus is illegal.

TOXICITY
Some people experience nausea soon after ingestion but the sensory changes begin after about 40 minutes and last for several hours. They are comparable with the symptoms of LSD (p. 33) and can lead to psychoses, flashbacks and blackouts.

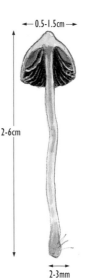

←— 0.5-1.5cm —→

2-6cm

2-3mm

HABITAT: Lawns, parks, playing fields and pastures. Not on dung.
FREQUENCY: Very common, often in large numbers especially after rain.
SEASON: Summer to autumn.
CAP: Bell-shaped but typically with a pointed umbo (as in the French 'liberty cap') and not expanding. Slimy and dark olive-brown when wet but drying to a pale straw colour. Margin slightly inrolled at first, later furrowed.
GILLS: Crowded, adnate or adnexed, ascending to the cap apex. Initially grey but maturing very dark brown with a white edge.
SPORE PRINT: Dark purple-brown (see picture).
STEM: Pale straw-coloured, very slender and rarely straight. Often becomes blue at the base when picked.
FLESH: Thin and pale. Strong smell when dry.

Clitocybe dealbata

Clitocybe rivulosa

Ivory Clitocybe or Sweating Mushroom

Clitocybe dealbata (Sow. ex Fr.) Kummer
and *Clitocybe rivulosa* (Per. ex Fr.) Kummer

TOXICITY

These two contain muscarine (see p. 21) which produces symptoms within 30 minutes. These include sickness, painful urination and profuse salivation and sweating. The latter can result in a weight loss of up to 4 kilos! Atropine, given under medical supervision, reverses the symptoms.

These 'little white jobs' are common in grassland and are frequently found with and collected in mistake for Fairy Ring Champignon (p. 66) and Snowy Waxcap (p. 63). The colour, decurrent gills and mealy smell of *C. dealbata* are also reminiscent of The Miller (p. 110). These two grassland Clitocybes and several related, small, white, woodland species are very poisonous and produce alarming symptoms, one being profuse sweating.

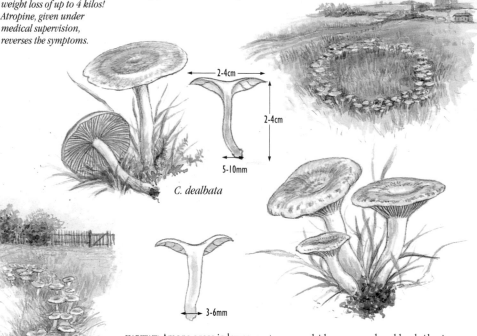

2-4cm

2-4cm

5-10mm

C. dealbata

3-6mm

HABITAT: Among grass in lawns, pastures, roadside verges and parkland. Also in mushroom and tomato beds.

FREQUENCY: Common, gregarious and often in fairy rings.

SEASON: Mid summer to late autumn.

CAP: For *C. dealbata* convex, becoming flattened and slightly depressed. Margin inrolled and wavy. Creamy grey to pale ochre with flesh tones. Dry and smooth. *C. rivulosa* as above but with a frosted surface and concentric buff zones.

GILLS: For *C. dealbata* crowded, adnate to shortly decurrent, white to grey-ochre. On *C. rivulosa* typically decurrent.

SPORE PRINT: White (see picture).

STEM: Smooth and white, tough but not pliable. More slender in *rivulosa*.

FLESH: For *C. dealbata* thin, white smelling mealy. *C. rivulosa* with a slight sweet smell or lacking smell.

Stinking Parasol

Lepiota cristata (Fr.) Kummer

The commonest of a range of small *Lepiota* species which are mistakenly consumed having been erroneously identified as small specimens of the edible Parasol Mushroom (p. 58). Although not deadly, some of its close relatives are and it serves as a type to be given a wide berth. All have small (<6 cm across) scaly caps, whitish free gills, white spores and a ring but no volva.

(p. 58)

POISONOUS
Lepiota cristata

TOXICITY
Lepiota cristata *is inedible and possibly poisonous. Related species (more common in the south) include some with a pleasant smell and darker scales which are very poisonous. The symptoms resemble those of the Death Cap (see p. 151) and include disruption of the nervous system.*

(see p. 151)

HABITAT: In short grass and leaf litter in woods, pastures, lawns and gardens.

FREQUENCY: Very common, usually gregarious.

SEASON: Summer to autumn.

CAP: Small, bell-shaped then flat with a broad umbo. White with a red-brown central patch surrounded by rings of similar coloured tiny scales.

GILLS: Very crowded, free and white – ageing brown.

SPORE PRINT: White (see picture).

STEM: Slender, fragile, silky white with a small transient ring and a pinkish base.

FLESH: Thin, white to pink. Strong, unpleasant smell, like coal-gas or rubber.

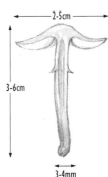

2-5cm

3-6cm

3-4mm

Edible Species in Broad-leaved Woodland

Woodland fungi include mycorrhizal, wood-rotting and litter decomposing species. Some fungal species occur in a wide range of different woodlands but others are very specific to just one or a restricted number of tree species. Good tree recognition can greatly ease the identification of woodland fungi. Not all trees have a rich associated fungal flora. The best species are beech, oak and birch. Included in this section are fungi that are associated with trees in parkland or hedges; a wood is not always required, a single tree can be sufficient.

83

The Russulas

There are over 100 species of Russula in Britain, many with brightly coloured caps and all associated with tree roots, some being specific to just one species (see p. 8). Typically with quite large, fleshy fruitbodies, they are all easily broken and can be crumbled, like good Cheshire cheese. With a white, cream or yellow spore print, most species lack intermediate gills and the family is easy to distinguish. Individual species are less readily identified, not least because they show enormous colour variation. Many are edible but of poor quality, though they are important food for slugs and other animals. There are several poisonous red species (see p. 178).

The Yellow Russulas:

Yellow Swamp Russula

Russula claroflava Grove

COOKING AND EATING
Opinions differ as to its culinary value but we enjoy it especially as it fruits early in the season. Wipe off any leaves stuck to the cap or peel it (the skin comes away easily) before sautéing with lemon juice.

This bright yellow species is worth looking for in damp birch woods from mid-summer onwards. There are several very common ochre-yellow species but these are easily distinguished by differences in colour, smell and habitat.

5-12cm

5-10cm

1-2cm

KEY FEATURES: Shiny, bright chrome-yellow cap with pale yellow gills. White stem bruising dark grey. Fruity smell and mild taste. Crumbly texture (common to all Russulas).

HABITAT: Wet ground under birch (or alder) and often among *Sphagnum* moss.
FREQUENCY: Frequent, more common in the north and west.
SEASON: Summer to early autumn (see histogram).
CAP: Chrome or buttercup yellow, paling with age, becoming shiny and slightly sticky; flat or depressed and with faint marginal grooves. Skin easily peels to half-way.
GILLS: Cream, ageing pale yellow.
SPORE PRINT: Ochre-yellow (see picture).
STEM: White, with patches of dark grey when bruised or old. Pale yellow at the base.
FLESH: White, exposed stem flesh turns grey; strong fruity smell and a mild taste (young specimens are slightly peppery).

J
F
M
A
M
J 🍄
J 🍄
A 🍄🍄🍄🍄🍄🍄
S 🍄🍄🍄🍄🍄🍄
O 🍄🍄🍄🍄🍄
N 🍄
D

LOOKALIKES

Russula ochroleuca – **Common Yellow Russula**
A very common fungus; it is distinguished by the more ochre-yellow cap, white stem flushed with the cap colour and greying with age. Pale cream gills and spore print. Flesh mild to moderately hot, hence not highly rated. Also in coniferous woods.

Russula lutea
Confusable with *ochroleuca* from above, but smaller (cap 3–7 cm) and with apricot-coloured gills, an ochre-yellow spore print and a strong smell of fruit or boiled sweets. Taste mild; edible but not worthwhile.

Russula fellea – **Geranium-scented Russula**
With beech, common. Uniform, dull, ochre-coloured cap, stem and gills – no greying. Pale cream spore print. White flesh smelling fruity or of geraniums (*Pelargonium*) and tasting hot, so not good to eat.

Green-Cracking or Sea Green Russula
Russula virescens (Schaeff. ex Zant.) Fr.

The most highly regarded of the edible Russulas and among the easiest to identify, but not common in Britain.

COOKING AND EATING
Many rate this the equal of Cep (p. 92); sadly the maggots also appreciate it! It is especially good fried or grilled – it can become soggy if cooked for too long. Best eaten fresh but it can be dried.

4-9cm

4-9cm

2-3cm

KEY FEATURES: Cap skin generally sea-green with patches of dark green, cream and ochre; cracking into small platelets revealing the white flesh and resulting in a mouldy appearance. Stem, gills, flesh and spore print all white.

HABITAT: Open woodland, especially with beech or oak.

FREQUENCY: Occasional, more common in the south.

SEASON: Summer to early autumn.

CAP: Soon flattened, often depressed and with the margin downturned. The dry, mealy skin starts cream but matures pale green with areas of darker green and yellow-brown and cracks into a mosaic pattern, revealing the white flesh.

GILLS: Creamy-white (see picture).

SPORE PRINT: White (see picture).

STEM: Stocky, equal or decreasing to the base, white with some brown staining. (Stains bright pink when rubbed with ferrous sulphate, see p. 42.)

FLESH: White and crumbly with a smell of young hazelnuts and a taste like new potatoes.

LOOKALIKES

There are other green Russulas including:

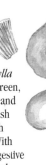

R. aeruginea
Similar to *heterophylla*
but cap more grey-green,
darker at the centre and
with forking, yellowish
gills. (Grey-pink with
ferrous sulphate.) With
birch. May cause digestive
upsets so best avoided.

R. heterophylla
With a smooth, yellow-green
cap and crowded, weakly
decurrent, forking white
gills. White stem (pinking
with ferrous sulphate).
Uncommon but edible
and good.

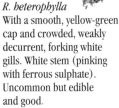

R. cutefracta
With a cracked, sometimes dark green skin
but colours include purple and bronze. (No
pinking with ferrous sulphate.) Edible.

Three other common, edible Russulas
occasionally produce green caps:

*R. cyanoxantha
var. peltereaui*
(see p. 88)

R. xerampelina
Dark green at the cap
middle, cross-veined,
pale ochre gills and a
pink flush to the white
stem which bruises
brown. Smelling and
tasting of shellfish.

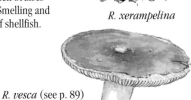

R. xerampelina

When collecting green
Russulas beware:

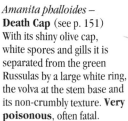

R. vesca (see p. 89)

Amanita phalloides –
Death Cap (see p. 151)
With its shiny olive cap,
white spores and gills it is
separated from the green
Russulas by a large white ring,
the volva at the stem base and
its non-crumbly texture. **Very
poisonous**, often fatal.

87

The Charcoal Burner

Russula cyanoxantha (Schaeff. ex Secr.) Fr.

COOKING AND EATING
Slugs and other animals usually get to the older ones but as it often appears in large numbers the older caps can be discarded. The young caps and stems are firm and fleshy and are best sliced and fried with plenty of lemon juice, garlic or other seasoning. Alternatively, mix with a stronger flavoured species or some dried ground Cep.

The specific Latin name refers to blue and yellow while the curious English name relates not to the method of cooking but to the colour range on a single cap, reminiscent of the colours in charcoal flame. One of the commonest Russulas, its many hues cause confusion for beginners. Its firm, thick flesh makes up for its mild flavour.

J
F
M
A
M ☂
J ☂☂
J ☂
A ☂☂☂☂
S ☂☂☂☂☂☂☂
O ☂☂☂☂☂
N ☂
D

KEY FEATURES: Firm cap with mix of colours including a selection of purple, grey, blue green and yellow. White gills unusually elastic for a Russula. White stem and flesh, the latter with little smell or taste. White spores. Crumbly texture of stem and cap flesh (Russula feature).

HABITAT: In all broad-leaved woods, especially with beech.

FREQUENCY: Very common.

SEASON: Summer to late autumn (see histogram).

CAP: Initially convex, later flat and often depressed. Firm, fleshy, smooth and shiny. Colour very variable – typically a blend including purple, blue and grey with yellow, brown and green nearer the centre. Some varieties are predominantly green (*peltereaui*, see p. 87) or yellow (*chlora*).

GILLS: Crowded, white, forked, greasy and pliable (not brittle).

SPORE PRINT: White (see picture).

STEM: Equal, firm but crumbly, smooth and white.

FLESH: Firm and thick, flushed red below the cap skin, elsewhere remaining white. No distinctive smell, mild taste.

LOOKALIKES

The pliable gills and mix of colours should distinguish the
Charcoal Burner from other Russulas, but it may be mistaken for:

Russula langei
Very similar but with cream gills and
usually a purple flush to the stem.
Edible and equally good.

Russula fragilis
With a blend of pink and
purple but only half the
size, less fleshy and quite
fragile. The cap has a
grooved margin, the gills
a toothed edge and the
fruity-smelling flesh is
very acrid, rendering it
inedible.

Russula parazurea
With a more grey-blue, scurfy cap, cream gills and pale
yellow flesh. Edible. Often with lime.

Russula nigricans – Blackening Russula
Mature specimens are nearly twice the size of the
Charcoal Burner with brown to black caps, stem
and gills. Young caps are dirty white, mottled with
brown and more readily confusable. The young gills are
straw-coloured and like the flesh turn red-pink when
damaged. Edible when young, before the maggots.

Russula vesca – Bare-toothed Russula
With a more wine-coloured cap; the common name
alludes to the retraction of the skin at the edges, showing
the flesh and gill tops – looking like teeth. White stem
tapering at the base with rusty spots which also develop
on the crowded, forked, white gills. Edible and good.

The Edible Milk Caps of Broad-leaved Woodland

These include: *Lactarius volemus* (Fr.) Fr.
Lactarius piperatus – Peppery Milk Cap
Lactarius glyciosmus – Coconut-scented Milk Cap
Lactarius camphoratus – Curry-scented Milk Cap

A long with the Russulas, the closely related Milk Caps form mycorrhizal associations with trees (see p. 8). Like the Russulas they have a brittle texture but differ in the latex ('milk') exuded from damaged gills and flesh, the decurrent gill attachment and typically less bright cap colours. Very few species are eaten in this country, probably because many have an acrid taste when raw, and also from earlier superstition about 'bleeding' fungi. Many more are consumed throughout the rest of Europe where even species described as poisonous in British books are eaten after careful preparation. The best-known edible species, *L. deliciosus,* is found in coniferous woods (see p. 166).

Lactarius volemus
Cap large, orange to red-brown, dry, with a suede-like feel. Stem thick, coloured as cap. Gills slightly decurrent, pale yellow, bruising brown and, when damaged, producing copious, mild-tasting white milk which stains the gills brown. White spore print. Creamy-yellow flesh 'milks', smells of shellfish and tastes of almonds. Edible and widely enjoyed on mainland Europe (salted and fried to add bulk to casseroles); much less common in Britain where it occurs mainly with oak.

A **lookalike** is the similarly coloured but much smaller *Lactarius rufus* – **Rufous Milk Cap**
Common beneath conifers or birch. The cap has a conical umbo and the white latex tastes very peppery; this has led to an inedible tag despite its use as a seasoning in eastern Europe.

Milk Caps used as seasoning include:

Lactarius glyciosmus – **Coconut-scented Milk Cap**
Small, flattened, depressed, grey-pink cap, downy when
young. Hollow stem as cap colour. Buff-yellow, crowded
gills. Creamy-yellow spores. White milk. Flesh smelling
of coconut, taste becoming slightly hot. With birch.

Lactarius camphoratus – **Curry-scented Milk Cap**
One of many small red-brown Milk Caps; identified by its
blunt umbo, stem and gills as cap colour, cream spores
and a watery, whey-like milk. Smelling oily when fresh,
old or dried specimens have a strong curry or chicory-
like smell. Dried and powdered it can be used as a curry
'spice'. Also found in coniferous woods.

Lactarius piperatus –
Peppery Milk Cap
Has a large, funnel-shaped,
ivory-white cap with an
incurved margin, very
crowded creamy-yellow gills
and acrid white milk. Small
amounts of cooked, fresh,
dried or salted specimens
may be used as a flavouring.

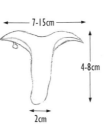

7-15cm

4-8cm

2cm

A **lookalike** is the even larger *Lactarius vellereus* with
cap to 20 cm and distant, white gills. Taste too acrid
even for use as a seasoning. Like *piperatus* it has white
spores and is frequent in the autumn.

Penny Bun or Cep

Boletus edulis Bull.

COOKING AND EATING
Young ones can be cooked or pickled whole (including the stem), they are also delicious sliced and eaten raw. With middle-aged ones twist off the stem, which should be peeled and sliced thinly to add to the cap. If the tubes are wet and olive coloured, pull them away from the flesh and discard. Sadly, older specimens are frequently maggot-ridden, especially in the stem. To dry, cut both cap and stem into chunks and thread them on string or a knitting needle above a radiator or in the airing cupboard. These can be reconstituted by soaking in warm water. Grind some to a powder which will add a wonderful flavour to any meal.

After the truffles this is Europe's most highly prized edible fungus. It is a good one for the beginner as it is easily distinguished from the few poisonous species found in the same family, it is common in Britain and one large specimen can provide the basis of a dish for four! Young ones can be pickled and a surfeit of larger ones is easily dried to provide year-round pleasure. They are sold fresh, dried and pickled.

8-30cm

5-25cm

<12cm

J
F
M
A
M
J
J
A
S
O
N
D

KEY FEATURES: Pores (the open ends of the tubes which take the place of gills in this and related species) white to pale straw, not discolouring on bruising; broad stem with pale raised honeycomb-like network only clearly visible near the cap.

HABITAT: Woodlands in general but with a preference for oak, beech, birch and pine. Often close to the edge of a wood or by paths and in grass where trees are present. The more conspicuous Fly Agaric (see p. 155), is a useful beacon for neighbouring ceps as the two are often found together.

FREQUENCY: Common, usually only a few together, but occasionally gregarious.

SEASON: Early summer to autumn (see histogram).

CAP: Starts smaller than the stem, deeply convex and covered with a white bloom. Mature caps are flat and various shades of brown or dirty white but paler towards the margin (like an old penny bun), sticky when wet and occasionally wrinkled.

PORES: Small, round, white, ageing to straw or light olive. Not changing when bruised.

TUBES: Free (stem and cap separate easily), colour as for pores.

SPORE PRINT: Olive brown (see picture).

STEM: Very swollen at the base in young specimens, pale brown and covered with a fine, white, raised honeycomb-like network which is more noticeable just below the cap.

FLESH: Thick, white, brown under skin, same on cutting. Pleasant smell, nutty taste.

LOOKALIKES

The only contenders are other members of the same family. Those with yellow, orange or red pores or with red on the stem are easily distinguished. This is fortunate as the only poisonous Boletes come in this group and include *Boletus erythropus, Boletus luridus,* and *Boletus satanus* (see pp. 159–160). Two very bitter-tasting species are *Boletus albidus (radicans),* with lemon-yellow pores and stem, and *Boletus calopus,* with pale yellow pores and a red stem.

Another common edible species which often grows in similar habitats to the Cep is:

Three less common species are similar to the Cep but as they are good to eat they do not pose a threat. They are:

Xerocomus badius – **Bay Bolete** (see p. 94)
From above it looks like a darker *edulis* but it has pale yellow pores which bruise blue-green and a more slender stem which lacks a raised network.

1. *Boletus reticulatus (aestivalis)*
The grey-brown cap cracks into a mosaic pattern and lacks the pale margin. Stem is covered by a white network which darkens with age. Early to mid summer with beech and oak.

2. *Boletus aereus*
Cap dark brown, pores and flesh white but bruising vinaceous, stem totally covered with a brown network. With beech and oak.

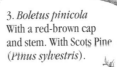

3. *Boletus pinicola*
With a red-brown cap and stem. With Scots Pine (*Pinus sylvestris*).

Tylopilus felleus – **Bitter Bolete**
With its brown cap, white pores and brown stem bearing a raised network, young specimens can easily be confused with the Cep but the pores bruise brown and the network is coarse, brown and visible all over the stem. In older specimens the pores have a pink tinge from the pink spores. The flesh is very bitter making it **inedible**.

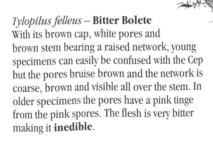

Bay Bolete

Xerocomus badius (Fr.) Kühn. ex Gilb. (*Boletus badius*)

COOKING AND EATING
Any leaves sticking to the cap should be wiped off prior to cooking. Cook as for Boletus edulis. *The stem is normally too fibrous and not worth cooking. Maggots are rare and it dries well.*

Similar in size to the Cep and often growing in the same localities, the Bay Bolete is common in Britain, appearing in large numbers after a wet summer. It is an excellent edible species with one great advantage over the Cep – it is only rarely maggot infested. Care must be taken not to confuse it with other species that blue on bruising as some of these are poisonous.

7-15cm

5-15cm

2-3cm

J
F
M
A
M
J
J
A
S
O
N
D

KEY FEATURES: Shiny bay-brown cap, yellow pores bruising blue-green, non-bulbous stem lacking network or black scales, flesh bluing slightly on cutting.

HABITAT: With both broad-leaved and coniferous trees on acid soils, favouring Scots Pine.

FREQUENCY: Common, singly or in groups.

SEASON Summer to autumn (see histogram).

CAP: The colour of a bay horse (or a horse chestnut), velvety when young and often sticky and darker after wet weather. Starts convex but flattens with age.

PORES: Clearly visible, angular. Cream then pale yellow and readily bruising a deep blue-green.

TUBES: Adnate to free, yellow to green, short and easily pulled from the flesh.

SPORE PRINT: Olive-brown (see picture).

STEM: Cylindrical lacking a bulbous base, but often curved, yellow-brown, frosted with brown streaks.

FLESH: Firm, pale yellow, slight bluing when cut. Mild smell, pleasant taste.

LOOKALIKES

Boletus edulis – **Penny Bun** (see p. 92)
Dark specimens can look like Bay Bolete from above but are distinguishable by the rounder, whiter pores, not bruising blue, and the bulbous stem with its white network on the upper portion. Edible and good.

Three common, yellow-brown capped Boletes with yellow or orange-red pores which bruise blue are:

Boletus erythropus – **Dotted-stemmed Bolete**
Common in woods on acid soils, this large fungus (cap to 20 cm) has a broad yellow stem covered with red dots, orange-red pores which bruise blue and yellow flesh (including in the stem) which blues instantly on cutting. Causes **digestive upsets** unless well cooked and even then some find it indigestible (see p. 160).

Xerocomus (Boletus) chrysenteron –
Red-cracked Bolete
A very common woodland species with a long fruiting season. Cap colour varies, but typically yellow-brown and cracking to reveal a pink-red layer. Pores large, angular, yellow to olive and readily bruising blue. Stem yellow, flushed with red. Edible but soggy and often maggoty or with a parasitic thread fungus on the pores.

Xerocomus (Boletus) subtomentosus –
Yellow-cracked Bolete
Easily confused with *chrysenteron* but the cracks on the cap reveal a yellow layer. The large, angular, golden-yellow pores barely blue on bruising and the stem is not red-tinted. Edible but soft and not worthwhile.

95

Orange Birch Bolete

Leccinum versipelle (Fr. & Hok) Snell

W ith its large orange cap and long stalk, this striking fungus fruits from early summer, has a very restricted habitat (look for it under birch trees) and the only lookalike species are also edible. While not competing with Cep for flavour, its cooked flesh is much firmer.

COOKING AND EATING
Older specimens have woody stems and spongy tubes (which should be discarded) but everything can be eaten in younger ones after removing the stem scales. During cooking the cap flesh turns dark grey – this is final proof of identification.

15–25cm

15–25cm

3–4cm

J
F
M
A
M
J 🍄🍄
J 🍄🍄
A 🍄🍄🍄
S 🍄🍄🍄🍄🍄🍄
O 🍄🍄🍄🍄🍄🍄
N 🍄
D 🍄

KEY FEATURES: Large orange cap. Small grey pores, white stem covered in small black scales. Cut flesh turning blue-grey then black. Growing with birch.

HABITAT: In open birch (or poplar) woodland often among bracken.

FREQUENCY: Common; finding one makes a search for more worthwhile.

SEASON: Early summer to autumn; in sudden flushes after rain (see histogram).

CAP: Very rounded, firm and brick-red when young. Expanding to a large, dry, orange-brown convex cap with overhanging shaggy margins.

PORES: Small, round, dirty white to grey, becoming pale brown.

TUBES: Grey, adnexed.

SPORE PRINT: Brown (see picture).

STEM: Long, tapering from the swollen base (which is often discoloured blue-green), white covered with small brown or black scales in longitudinal rows (hence old name, Rough Legs).

FLESH: Very thick, white or pale pink and firm but going blue-grey on cutting. Stem flesh becoming fibrous and sometimes bluing at base.

LOOKALIKES

There are a number of other edible *Leccinum* species, all with small scales on the stem:

Leccinum quercinum
Differs in its red-brown cap and stem scales. Found with oak in the south; not common. Edible.

Leccinum scabrum –
Brown Birch Bolete (see p. 98)
Common in birch woods and often growing with *L. versipelle*. Like a smaller, brown-capped version lacking the overhanging margin, with pores bruising brown and cut flesh not changing colour. Edible but less good.

Leccinum aurantiacum
Similar to *quercinum* but with aspen; not common. Edible.

The other lookalikes are the yellow-orange species of *Suillus* but these have a glutinous cap, lack the stem scales and are associated with conifers e.g.

Suillus grevillei – **Larch Bolete** (see p. 172)
Half the size of *L. versipelle* and always with larch. Edible.

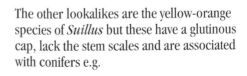

Brown Birch Bolete

Leccinum scabrum (Fr.) S. F. Gray

COOKING AND EATING
Use only young, firm-fleshed specimens and preferably discard the tubes (they separate easily from the flesh). Best for soups and stews.

Our commonest *Leccinum* and like *L. versipelle* it is associated with birch woods where the two are often found together. Many beginners think it is a small brown variety of *L. versipelle*. Sadly it is of poorer eating quality, with all but the very young ones becoming soggy and maggot-ridden.

5-10cm

8-15cm

2-3cm

J
F
M
A
M
J
J
A
S
O
N
D

KEY FEATURES: Medium sized brown cap, sticky in wet weather and soon becoming spongy. Small grey pores bruising brown. Slim white stem covered with tiny brown-black scales, denser near the base.

HABITAT: With birch trees.

FREQUENCY: Very common, often locally abundant.

SEASON: Early summer to autumn (see histogram).

CAP: Pale to grey-brown, convex and firm then flattening and becoming soft to the touch. No overhanging margin. Sticky (but not slimy) in wet weather.

PORES: Very small, grey and bruising dingy brown.

TUBES: Dirty white, almost free with a moat of shorter tubes surrounding the stem.

SPORE PRINT: Snuff brown (see picture).

STEM: Tapering from the base, white, covered with tiny brown-black scales, sparser near the top.

FLESH: Thick, soft, white, unchanging or faint pinking on cutting. Pleasant smell.

98

Leccinum versipelle –
Orange Birch Bolete
(see p. 96)
Also with birch but with a
larger, orange cap with an
overhanging margin. The
cut flesh turns grey-blue
and blackens on cooking.
Edible and good.

A number of other less common *Leccinum*
species (all with stem scales) also associated
with birch include:

L. variicolor with a mottled grey cap, pink flesh and the
basal stem flesh bluing. Edible.

L. roseofractum with a darker brown cap and flesh
turning rosy pink on cutting. Edible but poor.

L. holopus with a very pale
cap, growing in *Sphagnum*
moss. Edible but poor.

There are some brown-capped species of
Boletus (see pp. 92–93) but these lack the
stem scales while the brown-capped species
of *Suillus* (see pp. 170–171) have slimy caps,
no scales and are associated with conifers.

99

EDIBLE
Clitocybe odora

Aniseed Toadstool or *Blue-green Clitocybe*

Clitocybe odora (Bull. ex Fr.) Kummer

COOKING AND EATING
Cut the cap and stem into small pieces and dry. As with many spices the flavour is enhanced on drying. Add dried pieces (or powder) to dishes in place of anise or serve with fish in place of fennel.

Most of the edible fungi described in this book provide the basis for a side dish or a main meal but the Aniseed Toadstool is used purely as a flavouring, comparable with aniseed or fennel. The combination of an overall greenish-blue colour and a strong aniseed smell make this species unmistakable but there are fungi of the same colour and others with the same smell.

3-6cm

4-8cm

5-8mm

J
F
M
A
M
J
J
A 🍄🍄🍄
S 🍄🍄
O 🍄🍄🍄🍄🍄🍄🍄🍄🍄🍄🍄🍄🍄
N 🍄
D

KEY FEATURES: Small to medium-sized cap, blue-green especially when young, stem and gills a similar colour but slightly paler. Weakly decurrent gills and white spores. Strong smell of aniseed or fennel.

HABITAT: Among leaf litter, especially with beech and oak on calcareous soils.

FREQUENCY: Occasional, singly or in small groups.

SEASON: Late summer to autumn (see histogram).

CAP: Convex to flat, margin inrolled when young, later wavy; smooth and matt. Greenish-blue when young, becoming grey-green and finally almost cream on drying.

GILLS: Adnate to slightly decurrent, crowded. Cream when young, later grey-green.

SPORE PRINT: Creamy-white (see picture).

STEM: Slender, base thicker and with white down, flushed with cap colour.

FLESH: Thin, soft, white to pale green. Strong smell and mild taste of aniseed.

LOOKALIKES

The only species with a comparable **colour** is the **Verdigris Agaric** (actually two closely related species):

Stropharia aeruginosa and *Stropharia caerulea*
Common species of grassland or open woodland with smaller, more bell-shaped, blue-green caps, sticky when young, brown, pale-edged gills and purple-black spores. Scaly stem below the ring. **Poisonous**.

Several of the larger woodland *Clitocybe* species are also edible, **but not to everyone**:

Other species **smell** of aniseed including:

Clitocybe fragrans
A woodland species with a smaller, depressed cap and long thin stem. Pale yellow-brown cap with flesh-coloured gills. Edible but too easily confused with some of the creamy-tan, highly poisonous species such as *Clitocybe dealbata* and *C. rivulosa* (see p. 80). **So do not risk eating**.

Clitocybe clavipes – **Club-footed Funnel Cap**
Grey-brown cap (5–10 cm) shaped like an inverted cone, pale yellow decurrent gills and a stem with a very swollen base. Unpleasant smell. Edible but **causes alarming symptoms with alcohol** in a manner similar to the Common Ink Cap (see p. 20).

Clitocybe nebularis – **The Clouded Agaric**
A large (cap to 20 cm), fleshy, funnel-shaped, grey-coloured fungus, common in both broad-leaved and coniferous woodland; often in rings. Young specimens are tasty to some, but others find them indigestible and a few develop headaches and skin allergies; it is **to be avoided**.

Wood Blewit or *Blue Stalks*

Lepista nuda (Bull. ex Fr.) Cooke *(Tricholoma nudum)*

A close relative of the grassland species *L. saeva* (see p. 64), this more common species is typically associated with woodlands. Apart from its violet hue it is unusual in that it continues fruiting to Christmas and beyond, considerably extending the season for edibles. It is still collected and sold in markets in the Midlands, its pleasant aroma and thick flesh putting a price on its head. Wood Blewit is, however, frequently confused with other species, some of which are poisonous and have been sold as 'Blewits'.

COOKING AND EATING
Best eaten young as older ones become watery and maggoty, with tough stems. The strong flavour makes this a good stewing fungus and as it keeps much of its colour when fried it is an attractive addition to any meal. Wood Blewit should not be eaten raw as it may be slightly poisonous to some people unless well cooked.

5-15cm

5-10cm

1.5-2.5cm

J
F
M
A
M
J
J
A
S
O
N
D

KEY FEATURES: Medium to large, thick, violet to tan cap with incurved margin. Gills sinuate, crowded, lilac to buff. Spore print pale pink. Stem fleshy, violet, fading paler.
HABITAT: Among herbs or in grass in woodlands (including conifers), hedges and parks. In leaf litter or compost in gardens.
FREQUENCY: Common. Gregarious, sometimes in rings.
SEASON: Autumn to late winter (see histogram).
CAP: Convex, expanding to flat or depressed with incurved, wavy margin. Fleshy, smooth, slightly viscid when moist. Colour varies from blue-violet to tan, the latter especially in the centre and with age.
GILLS: Sinuate, crowded, lilac becoming pink-brown. Easily separated from the flesh.
SPORE PRINT: Pale pink (see picture).
STEM: Violet, with white fibrils, mostly at the apex. Paling with age. Solid, equal or with a bulbous base.
FLESH: Thick at the centre with a violet tinge above the gills. Watery after wet weather. Smell and taste fruity.

Lookalikes

Two closely related, edible species are:

Lepista sordida
In similar habitats to
L. nuda but uncommon
and distinguishable by its
smaller size, flesh-brown
cap and stem, pale lilac-
pink gills and faint
cyanide smell.

Lepista saeva – **Field Blewit** (see p. 64)
In grassland, parkland and woodland margins; less
common. Distinguished by the lack of violet on the
cap and gills and the stockier stem with bright lilac
longitudinal streaks on a white background.

A number of other woodland species have
violet on the cap, stem or gills; several are in
the genus *Cortinarius*. The following three
species are eaten in parts of Europe but there
are hundreds of *Cortinarius* species, many
are easily confused, and some are deadly
poisonous. We have had reports of severe
digestive upsets following the accidental
ingestion of *C. purpurascens*. **Avoid
species with brown spores**.

Cortinarius violaceus
Of a similar size and with
a dark violet cap, stem
and gills; uncommon.
Look for the cobweb-like
veil protecting the gills in
young specimens and the
rusty-brown spore print.

Cortinarius purpurascens
A much commoner species differing in the more purple-
brown cap. Sometimes grows with Wood Blewit and is
easily mistaken for it (it even has a fruity smell) but it
has rusty-brown spores and purple flesh, especially in
the stem.

Cortinarius largus
With a pale lilac-blue to brown cap and stem and pale
blue gills this occasional species has rusty-brown
spores.

Wood Blewit when seen from above may be confused with some of the purple-coloured species of *Russula* e.g.

Russula cyanoxantha –
Charcoal Burner (see p. 88)
Easily distinguished by its white gills and stem and by the crumbly texture, common to all *Russulas*. This species is edible but many *Russulas* are not.

Three much smaller species with violet or lilac cap (<5 cm) and stem are:

Inocybe geophylla var. *lilacina*
With an umbonate cap and a cobweb-like veil protecting the young adnate gills which mature clay-brown (as the spore colour). Common especially by woodland paths. **Very poisonous**.

Laccaria amethystea –
Amethyst Deceiver
(see p. 113)
With violet cap, stem and widely-spaced gills (adnate to decurrent) best distinguished by its small size, thin stem and white spores. Common, often with beech litter. Edible.

Mycena pura
With a lilac or pink-grey cap, stem and gills, the latter are adnate with a white edge. The stem is hollow and often twisted. White spore print. Smells of radish. Common in leaf litter. **Poisonous** (contains muscarine).

Bleeding Brown Mushroom

Agaricus haemorrhoidarius Schulz. ap. Kalchbr.

T he Mushroom of broad-leaved woods where its brown cap is well camouflaged among soil and dead leaves. With a stem and gills that bruise red and cut flesh that becomes blood-red it is not for the faint hearted! It is in fact edible and good to eat.

COOKING AND EATING
Comparable with Field Mushroom (p. 47) and Brown Wood Mushroom (p. 168) but less juicy.

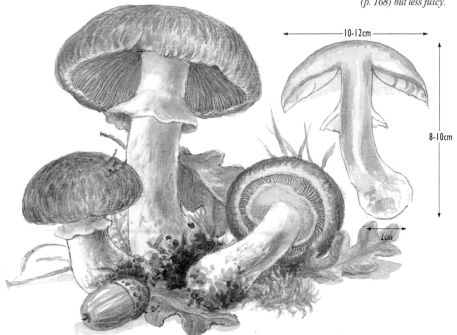

← 10-12cm →

8-10cm

2cm

KEY FEATURES: Hazel-brown cap with flesh-pink gills. Long, stout stem, bruising red, with double ring and bulbous base. Gills and cut flesh turning blood-red. With broad-leaved trees.

HABITAT: With broad-leaved trees, especially oak.

FREQUENCY: Fairly common but rarely in large numbers.

SEASON: Autumn (see histogram).

CAP: Hazel-brown, the surface faintly breaking up into scales.

GILLS: Enclosed in a white veil and deep pink when young. Becoming darker and bruising red. Free.

SPORE PRINT: Very dark brown (see picture).

STEM: Long, stout, hollow, with bulbous base. Long, floppy, double ring that is brown underneath. Lower stem region covered with small white scales.

FLESH: White, changing immediately blood-red on cutting. Thick. Smell faint.

J
F
M
A
M
J
J
A
S
O ⬤⬤⬤⬤⬤⬤⬤⬤⬤⬤⬤⬤⬤⬤
N
D

LOOKALIKES

Confusion is most likely with other *Agaricus* (Mushroom) species, most of which are edible.

The most similar looking species is:
A. silvaticus – **Brown Wood Mushroom**
This has a slimmer stem and is found with conifers (see p. 168). Edible.

A. lanipes
Occasional with beech and oak. Cap covered with large chocolate-brown scales. Stem short, club-shaped and very broad at the base which is encircled by brown scales. Stem flesh pinking at apex, more orange at base. Sweet smell. Edible but not worthwhile.

A. praeclaresquamosus (placomyces)
With broad-leaved trees, uncommon and with the cap covered in small concentrically arranged dark scales. White stem, ring and flesh in stem base all stain yellow on bruising. Smells of Indian ink.
Probably poisonous and best avoided.

A. augustus –
The Prince
In grass under various trees, not common. The large, scaly cap stains deep yellow on bruising; the margins have overhanging veil remnants. Stem bruises yellow. Flesh does not redden and smells of almonds. Edible and excellent.

Another possible source of confusion is:

A. romagnesii
Habitat as above. Mature cap with central depression, with hazel-brown scales on a paler background. Stem base bruising yellow and tapering into thick mycelial strands. Ring thin, not permanent. White flesh only faintly flushing in stem apex. Faint smell of carbolic.
Probably poisonous and best avoided.

Cystolepiota aspera (Lepiota freisii)
Brown cap covered in pointed scales, distinguished by its white, often forked gills, white spore print and rubber-smelling flesh. Edibility unknown, so avoid.

Wood Mushroom

Agaricus silvicola (Vitt.) Sacc.

COOKING AND EATING
Similar to Horse Mushroom though much less substantial and with a stronger taste of aniseed. Singer (1975) reports that some people suffer digestive upset similar to that from Yellow-staining Mushroom.

Unlike the two other woodland mushrooms (*A. silvaticus*, p. 168, *A. haemorrhoidarius*, p. 105) this white-capped species is more comparable with the grassland species and is sometimes mistaken for a small Horse Mushroom (see p. 50). Unfortunately it yellows in a similar way to the poisonous Yellow-staining Mushroom (p. 78), and it has been confused with the deadly Destroying Angel (p. 152) so if in doubt check their descriptions; if still in doubt, discard.

KEY FEATURES: Cap and stem white but yellowing on bruising. Slender stem with bulbous base. Young gills pinkish-grey before maturing dark brown. Flesh smells of aniseed.
HABITAT: On soil in both broad-leaved and coniferous woods.
FREQUENCY: Occasional, usually in small groups.
SEASON: Autumn.
CAP: Convex but soon flattening, thin-fleshed. Smooth and initially creamy-white but ageing and bruising slowly to yellow-ochre.
GILLS: Enclosed in a white veil and grey-pink when young, maturing dark brown. Crowded, free.
SPORE PRINT: Very dark brown (see picture).
STEM: Slender, smooth and as cap colour. Not tapering but with a bulbous base, hollow. Pendulous, single-layered ring often torn, white above, darker beneath.
FLESH: Thin. White but yellow beneath cap skin and becoming dark brown at stem base. Aniseed smell.

Agaricus arvensis –
Horse Mushroom (see p. 50)
Also smells of aniseed but is a much more
robust, grassland species up to twice the size
and with a two-layered ring. Slight patchy
yellowing with age. Edible and good.

Agaricus macrosporus
Also smells of aniseed but the large cap remains convex
and the stem is stout with tiny scales below the ring. Cut
flesh in stem base pinking. In grassland, more frequent
in the north. Edible and good.

Amanita virosa –
Destroying Angel
(see p. 152)
Distinguished by its white,
sack-like basal volva,
white gills and spore
print, grooved ring and a
sickly sweet smell. With
broad-leaved trees.
Deadly poisonous.

Agaricus xanthodermus –
Yellow-staining Mushroom (see p. 78)
Distinguished by the flattened top to the button stage,
cap margin and stem quickly bruising bright yellow, cut
flesh in stem base bright chrome-yellow and with an
unpleasant ink-like smell. **Poisonous** to some, causing
sickness and diarrhoea for several days.

The Miller

Clitopilus prunulus (Scop. ex Fr.) Kummer

At a recent fungal fry-up, The Miller was voted the tastiest from a selection including the traditionally much more highly acclaimed Cep and Chanterelle. Its exclusion from some gastronomic guides may be because it is rarely found in large numbers and care must be taken not to collect the poisonous white Clitocybes; but those who enjoy a mealy meal, read on.

COOKING AND EATING

Said to have a resemblance to sweetbreads when prepared for the table, but do not be put off by this! At their best when fried in butter and eaten on toast. They need very little seasoning, save some lemon juice. Worth drying if enough can be found.

J
F
M
A
M
J
J
A
S
O
N
D

KEY FEATURES: Creamy white, flat or depressed cap with the feel of kid gloves and a strong smell of fresh meal. Mature gills flesh-coloured, strongly decurrent on to an often off-centred stem. Pink spore print.

HABITAT: Among grass, in parkland or among leaf-litter in open woodland (often with beech).

FREQUENCY: Common, usually in small groups.

SEASON: Late summer to autumn (see histogram).

CAP: Creamy white to grey, initially convex with an inrolled margin later becoming flat and depressed, often with a wavy edge. Dry and with the feel of kid leather.

GILLS: Strongly decurrent. Changing from white to pink with age.

SPORE PRINT: Pink (see picture).

STEM: Not always central, short, white and solid.

FLESH: White and firm. Smelling and tasting strongly of freshly milled flour.

4-10cm

3-6cm

5-10mm

LOOKALIKES

Calocybe gambosa – **St George's Mushroom** (see p. 52)
Also with a mealy smell. More common in grassland where it fruits in late spring, it is distinguished by being white all over, with a white spore print, sinuate gills and a fleshier cap and stem. Edible and good with a firm texture.

Entoloma lividum –
Livid Entoloma (see p. 76)
Uncommon but in the same habitat as The Miller and also with an inrolled, wavy edge to the cap, flesh-coloured mature gills and pink spores. Distinguishable by its larger size, thick stem, dirty-white cap and sinuate gills. **Poisonous**, causing severe gastric upsets and possible liver damage.

Clitocybe dealbata – **Ivory Clitocybe** (see p. 80)
Common in grassy places, often in rings. Very similar but slightly smaller, with a glossy cap surface and creamy-coloured gills only slightly decurrent, and with white spores. Contains muscarine and **can be fatal**. There are a number of larger, white *Clitocybe* species with a mealy smell. All have white spores. **Avoid**.

The Deceiver

Laccaria laccata (Scop. ex Fr.) Cooke

COOKING AND EATING
The thin caps are rarely maggot-infested and large numbers can be quickly gathered. Discard the tough stems. Firm textured but lacking flavour so best in stews, soups and sauces, or with a stronger flavoured fungus, e.g. Shaggy Ink Cap.

O ne of the most common toadstools but among the most variable, hence its common name. Beginners often find it difficult to identify because of its variability. Despite this it is clearly distinguishable from the many other 'little brown jobs'. While not a gourmet species, its abundance, even in dry spells, makes it a useful standby. It is often found with its close relative, Amethyst Deceiver, which is also edible.

1-4cm

3-10cm

25-50mm

J
F
M
A
M
J ☂
J ☂☂☂
A ☂☂☂☂☂☂☂☂☂
S ☂☂☂☂☂☂☂☂☂
O ☂
N
D

KEY FEATURES: Cap small, flat, slightly depressed and scurfy in the centre. Dull, moist, date-brown, drying pale beige. Thin, fibrous, concolorous stem, very variable in length. Thick, very widely-spaced flesh-coloured gills, adnate to slightly decurrent. White spores.
HABITAT: With both broad-leaved and coniferous trees, amongst the litter.
FREQUENCY: Very common, often in large numbers.
SEASON: Late summer to autumn (see histogram).
CAP: Soon flattening, slightly depressed and scurfy in the centre, wavy and striate (when moist) at the margin. Red-brown, often with flesh tints, but drying yellow-brown.
GILLS: Adnate or slightly decurrent, thick and widely-spaced; flesh-coloured, maturing pinkish-brown with white spore dust.
SPORE PRINT: White (see picture).
STEM: Length varies from four times to only half the cap diameter. Thin, fibrous, cap-coloured; often twisted or bent.
FLESH: Thin, red-brown, odourless and with little taste.

LOOKALIKES

There are many small, brown-capped, **white-spored** woodland fungi including:

Collybia species – with pliable stems and crowded gills. Inedible.

Mycena species – tiny, delicate, bell-shaped fungi. Mostly inedible.

e.g. *Mycena sanguinolenta*

e.g. *Collybia dryophila* – **Russet Tough-shank**

A related species can be confusing when old and dry:

Be careful not to confuse other small, purple-coloured fungi with Amethyst Deceiver such as:

Laccaria amethystea –
Amethyst Deceiver
Equally common especially under beech. Very similar in all its features except colour which is violet in young moist caps, stems and gills but fades to light ochre with only a hint of violet. Edibility as *L. laccata* but with the advantage that it adds colour!

Mycena pura
This is typically a rosy-lilac colour, has pinkish-grey gills and smells of radish. **Poisonous**.

Inocybe geophylla var *lilacina*
This **very poisonous** species has an umbonate cap, crowded, **brown gills** and a brown spore print.

Chanterelle
Cantharellus cibarius Fr.

COOKING AND EATING
Slice larger specimens before frying. Add garlic, parsley or lemon juice. Excellent in omelettes. Can be eaten raw. Good for pickling but does not freeze or dry well. Rarely infected with maggots but soil needs to be removed with a damp cloth.

One of the best-known of all the edible fungi and extensively eaten throughout mainland Europe where it is commonly sold in local markets. Despite this a number of other species are frequently mistaken for it and consumed in error.

J
F
M
A
M
J
J 🍄🍄
A
S 🍄🍄🍄🍄🍄🍄🍄🍄🍄🍄🍄🍄
O 🍄🍄🍄🍄🍄
N
D

2-10cm

2-8cm

<2cm

KEY FEATURES: Funnel-shaped cap lacking true gills, faint smell of apricots and overall egg-yolk yellow colour. There are two edible species in the same genus. *C. tubaeformis* has a browner cap and hollow stem, whereas *C. lutescens* is more orange in colour with a hollow stem.

HABITAT: Woodland, usually broad-leaved (especially beech or oak) but sometimes pine and birch particularly in Scotland. Grows where plant cover is sparse, often amongst moss on sloping ground.

FREQUENCY: Singly or in troops, locally common.

SEASON: Summer and autumn (see histogram).

CAP: Convex when young, then flattening and becoming funnel-shaped, with a central depression. Thick-fleshed, dry on top with a blunt edge, slightly inrolled when young, later becoming irregularly wavy. The skin does not peel and is an egg-yolk yellow colour, fading with age.

GILLS: No true gills, but a network of distant wrinkles or veins, rarely more than 2 mm deep, blunt-edged, forking and reuniting in an irregular fashion. Their decurrent nature gives the appearance of fan vaulting. They are concolorous with the cap.

SPORE PRINT: Pale ochre-yellow (see picture).

STEM: Fleshy, solid, broadest at the top and gradually decreasing to the base. Colour slightly paler than the cap.

FLESH: Pale yellow with no change on cutting or bruising. Faint fruity smell as of apricots. Mild peppery aftertaste when eaten raw.

LOOKALIKES

Hygrophoropsis aurantiaca –
False Chanterelle (see p. 177)
More frequent with conifers and on
heathland. Thin cap with inrolled
margin. True, crowded, forking gills
(not reuniting). Thin stem. More
orange in colour and lacking the
fruity smell. **Poisonous to a
minority**, not worthwhile to others.

Hygrocybe pratensis –
Meadow Waxcap
(see p. 61)
A grassland species with
thick waxy gills. Edible
and good.

Hydnum repandum – **Hedgehog Fungus** (see p. 118)
Very similar when seen from above and often growing
with Chanterelle but the spores are borne on peg-like
projections. Edible and good. Under broad-leaved trees,
especially beech, often in moss.

*Cortinarius
speciossimus*

Two species of *Cortinarius*, both with adnate
gills, rusty-brown spores and cobweb-like veil
in young specimens. *C. orellanus* in southern
England and *C. speciossimus* in Scotland.
Both are rare but **very poisonous** (p. 19).

Omphalotus olearius – **Jack O'Lantern**
On trunks and buried roots of sweet chestnut (and oak)
in southern England. Very decurrent gills which glow in
the dark. Unpleasant smell. Very rare. **Poisonous**.

Horn of Plenty or Trumpet of Death
Craterellus cornucopioides (L.) Pers.

W ith its funereal name, drab colour and leathery texture this inconspicuous fungus does not strike one as a gourmet's treat, but expect to pay high prices for meals which include it – usually wrapped around a tasty stuffing. The only other species with the same overall size, shape and colour is also edible.

COOKING AND EATING
Check that the base is free of dirt and animal life. The caps should be gently sautéed until tender and then stuffed or used in soups or sauces. The taste is better than the texture and, as it dries well, it is worth grinding to a powder to use as a flavouring.

2-8cm

4-10cm

J
F
M
A
M
J
J
A
S 🍄🍄🍄🍄🍄🍄🍄🍄🍄🍄🍄
O 🍄🍄🍄🍄🍄🍄🍄🍄
N
D

KEY FEATURES: Trumpet shape; almost smooth, spore-bearing outer surface; brown-black colour.

HABITAT: Often hidden under leaf litter in oak or more particularly beech woods.

FREQUENCY: In groups, occasional.

SEASON: Summer to early winter (see histogram).

CAP: Trumpet- or funnel-shaped, hollow to the base and with an outrolled, wavy, split top. The inner surface of the 'horn' is a dingy brown.

GILLS: None – the spore-bearing outer surface of the cap is slightly ridged and almost black before the spores give it a grey-white bloom.

SPORE PRINT: White (see picture).

STEM: None or very short.

FLESH: Thin, grey and leathery with a slight smell and an earthy taste when eaten raw.

LOOKALIKES

With its dark colour and distinctive shape, few species can be confused with this species.

Cantharellus cinereus
Similar in size, shape and colour but the spores are borne on wrinkles (as in Chanterelle, see p. 114). Uncommon in deciduous woods. Edible.

<20cm

Russula nigricans –
Blackening Russula (see p. 89)
Old specimens go black, hard and funnel-shaped but this is a much larger fungus (cap up to 20 cm) with a separate stem and true gills. Edible when young.

Hedgehog Fungus
Hydnum repandum L. ex Fr.

COOKING AND EATING
The slight bitterness disappears on cooking but as a precaution blanch prior to cooking. Very rarely insect-infested and any dirt in the spines can be removed with a knife. With old specimens, remove the spines. We prefer this to Chanterelle as it has a firmer texture. It is worth serving on its own, sliced and lightly fried. It can be pickled, dried and even freezes well (cook first).

F or those interested in edible fungi it is reassuring to know that the only common toadstool with teeth is edible and excellent, being sold in most European countries. Some of the older books refer to two closely related species, the other being *Hydnum rufescens* but we shall follow the recent trend and consider *rufescens* as a variety of *H. repandum*. Fortunately they are both equally edible.

J
F
M
A
M
J
J
A
S
O
N
D

KEY FEATURES: Medium-sized, fleshy cap, cream to yellow-orange colour (smaller and orange-red in *rufescens*) often irregular. Stalactite-like spines in place of gills, crowded and decurrent (only slightly in *rufescens*). Short stem often excentric to the cap.
HABITAT: Under coniferous and broad-leaved trees, especially beech, often in moss.
FREQUENCY: Occasional but locally abundant, sometimes in rings.
SEASON: Autumn (see histogram).
CAP: Fleshy, matt, varying in colour from off-white through yellow to orange-red (var *rufescens*). Margin inrolled, wavy and frequently irregular when two or more caps grow in close proximity.
SPINES: Paler than cap, crowded, brittle, unequal in length, to 5 mm long, decurrent (less so in *rufescens*).
SPORE PRINT: White (see picture).
STEM: Short and stout (slender in *rufescens*). Often excentric to the cap and misshapen, paler than cap.
FLESH: Thick, brittle, pale yellow and with a pleasant smell. Older specimens have a slightly bitter taste when eaten raw.

Phellodon tomentosus
Less than half the size and with a zoned, brown cap, grey-brown, thin stem and grey spines this is an uncommon species of broad-leaved woods. Tough and inedible.

In the Scottish pine forests there are a number of spiny inedible species, typically smaller than *Hydnum* and with tough flesh. The only other edible one is:

Sarcodon imbricatum
Bigger than *Hydnum* and with the cap covered with rings of grey-brown scales.

From above the colour, size and shape is easily confused with:

Cantharellus cibarius – **Chanterelle** (see p. 114)
Easily separated by the absence of spines – the under-surface of the egg-yolk yellow cap has deep folds in place of gills. In similar habitats, edible and excellent.

Summer Truffle

Tuber aestivum Vitt.

COOKING AND EATING
Historically this species supported professional truffle hunters in Britain but its milder aroma is inferior to that of Perigord or Piedmont truffles. Carefully brush away any soil from the warty skin and slice thinly to add flavour to stuffings and patés. Add to omelettes or baked egg or simmer in dry white wine and eat on their own. Use fresh; they can be preserved in oil but this reduces their aroma and flavour.

Truffles are the most sought-after of all fungi and command a very high price. The two most valued species, the Perigord Truffle and Piedmont Truffle, are not found in Britain but the Summer Truffle is not uncommon, though rarely found. Underground fungi have long excited curiosity, not least as to their methods of reproduction and dispersal. Truffles produce spores inside the fruitbody and these are dispersed by animals, attracted to the truffles by their characteristic smell. Finding these buried fungi by chance is very unlikely and pigs and trained dogs have long been used to sniff them out. In parts of France and Italy truffle hunting is an important part of the local economy but there have been no professional hunters in Britain for 60 years.

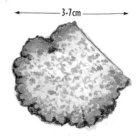

3-7cm

KEY FEATURES: The size and shape of a squash ball but looking like an old rounded pine cone with its covering of dark brown, pyramid-shaped warts. The pale flesh matures brown with white marbling and has a strong but pleasant smell.

HABITAT: Buried in the ground, sometimes just showing above the surface. Preferring chalk or limestone soils and mostly with beech.

FREQUENCY: Rarely found but probably not uncommon in the right habitats, especially in southern England.

SEASON: Late summer and autumn.

FRUITBODY: Rounded and hard with a brown-black knobbly skin produced by a regular pattern of pyramidal warts.

FLESH: Marbled, pale brown and white; the brown regions being the spore-bearing regions (spores yellowish brown). Strong, pleasant smell and a strangely nutty taste.

LOOKALIKES

Tuber brumale –
The Winter Truffle
Like a smaller version of
aestivum but with blue-
grey marbled flesh,
restricted to southern
England and not maturing
until early winter. Edible.

Tuber melanosporum –
**The Perigord or Black
Truffle**
Although not found in Britain
it is of similar size and shape
but the black warts are
grooved and polygonal in
shape, and the white areas
of the flesh turn reddish on
cutting. Associated with oak
and found through the winter
months.

←— 2-8cm —→

There are a number of other subterranean
fungi found in Britain which have sometimes
been used to adulterate truffles, the most
common being:

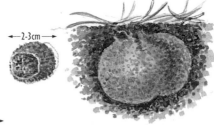

←—2-3cm—→

←——— 4-12cm ———→

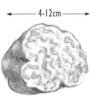

Elaphomyces granulatus – **False Truffle**
Smaller, with a pale brown outer skin covered in
small rounded warts and a thick, golden inner
skin surrounding the powdery grey-black spore
mass. In coniferous woods. Inedible.

Similar in size is the Red Truffle – *Tuber rufum*, with an
almost smooth, brown to red skin. Most common in the
south-west, where it was sold in the past.

Choiromyces meandraeformis – **False White Truffle**
Like a small potato with a yellow-brown smooth skin
and veined, creamy flesh with a very strong fruity smell.
Uncommon under broad-leaved trees. Edible but a poor
substitute for the similar looking *Tuber magnatum* –
the White or Piedmont truffle which is not found in
Britain.

←——— 3-12cm ———→

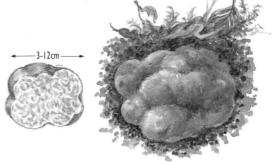

Although normally growing on soil in woods
the rounded fruitbodies of the earthballs
are sometimes half buried and have been
confused with and used to adulterate truffles:

Scleroderma citrinum and *Scleroderma verrucosum*
(see picture on p. 72)
Distinguishable from the Summer Truffle by their yellow-
brown colour and thick attaching threads and from the
true and false White Truffle by the thick skin and purple-
black spore mass. When young the flesh is marbled
and similar to the darker truffles. **Mildly poisonous**,
causing digestive upsets, especially if eaten raw.

Common morel
Morchella esculenta (L.) Pers.

J
F
M
A ⚬⚬⚬⚬⚬⚬⚬
M ⚬⚬⚬⚬⚬⚬⚬⚬⚬⚬⚬⚬⚬⚬
J
J
A
S
O
N
D

The morels (there are six closely related species or varieties) are the most sought-after of the spring fungi. Once discovered they can be collected from the same site annually – good sites are kept secret! Although they are easily distinguished from all the other edible fungi described in this book some similar species in the family *Helvellaceae* are poisonous if eaten raw and the false morel is **very** poisonous (see p. 124).

←—— 3-6cm ——→

3-10cm

2-3cm

COOKING AND EATING
Cut the stem base and check for intruders in the hollow chamber. Large specimens can be stuffed and baked but for other recipes cut longitudinally to aid cleaning and more even cooking. Morels are very easy to dry whole and can be reconstituted by soaking in water and milk. Morels dried and ground to a powder provide a wonderful flavouring. Long, slow cooking is advisable and they should not be eaten raw or in large quantity as some find them difficult to digest. Old specimens which may be mildewed must be avoided as there is growing evidence of poisoning similar to that from Gyromitra (see p. 19).

KEY FEATURES: Cap covered in deep honeycomb-like pits, not flattened or separate from the stem. Hollow cap and stem forming one continuous chamber, not subdivided. Brittle texture.

HABITAT: Well drained sandy, chalk or limestone soils or after fire. Under broad-leaved trees (especially ash and elm) in open woodland, in old hedges and in gardens.

FREQUENCY: Occasional but locally frequent.

SEASON: April to May, after rain (see histogram).

CAP: Very variable in shape and colour with some authors creating separate species for the variants (see lookalikes). Globular or egg-shaped and even conical; frequently non-symmetrical. Hollow. Surface covered in deep pits, like an untidy honeycomb, the pit colour ranging from light ochre to brown, grey and black. Darkening with age or after frost. Pit walls concolorous or paler.

SPORE PRINT: Creamy-yellow.

STEM: White to pale brown, grooved or wrinkled, fused to the cap. Hollow, the chamber being continuous with that of the cap.

FLESH: Thin and firm. Mushroom smell.

LOOKALIKES

Also edible and good are the following two species which are so similar to *esculenta* that they are often classed as variants:

Morchella rotunda
With a larger, broader, ochre-coloured cap, and the stem separated from the cap by an apical furrow. On heavier soils; fruiting later than *esculenta*.

Morchella vulgaris
This has grey-brown, sometimes compound pits with concolorous walls. On rich soil.

Two other edible species have narrow, spire-shaped caps:

Morchella conica (*M. elata*) – with longitudinally extended rectangular pits.

Morchella costata – with prominent longitudinal pit walls forming parallel ribs and less obvious horizontal walls.

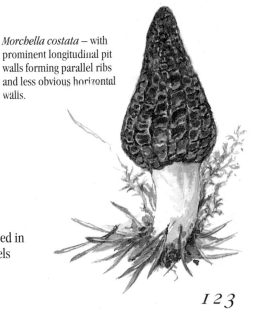

(Both of these species were discovered in a packet of commercially dried morels marked *Morchella conica!*)

One related species, also edible but less good is:

Mitrophora semilibera (M. hybrida)
Has a small cap with the lower part free of the long white mealy stem. In damp woods in late spring.

Two species in the family *Helvellaceae* are morel-like, but are **autumn** fruiting:

Helvella crispa
With a creamy-white, brittle, saddle-shaped, lobed cap and a hollow deeply grooved stem. Edible when cooked but chewy.

Helvella lacunosa – **Elfin's Saddle**
Similar to *H. crispa* but with a more lobed, grey to black cap. Said to be edible after boiling but **best avoided**.

There is unfortunately one **highly poisonous** spring-fruiting fungus that has been mistaken for a morel and has proved fatal (see p.19):

Gyromitra esculenta – **False Morel or Turban Fungus**
Rare in conifer woods. Cap is fist size, chestnut brown and deeply convoluted. The hollow broad stem is multi-chambered like the cap. Morels are single-chambered.

Puffballs of broad-leaved woodland

S ome puffballs are restricted to open habitats. The Giant Puffball (see p. 68) is more frequent in pastures and hedgerows but is also found in woodlands. The following are typically found in broad-leaved woodlands but may also occur with conifers. All puffballs are edible when white inside but some other ball-shaped fungi are not (see over).

(see p. 68)

EDIBLE

Lycoperdon pyriforme
Lycoperdon perlatum

COOKING AND EATING
Puffballs must be firm and white inside; do not eat them when the spore mass has turned brown. Spines can be wiped off and some may require peeling before slicing and frying.

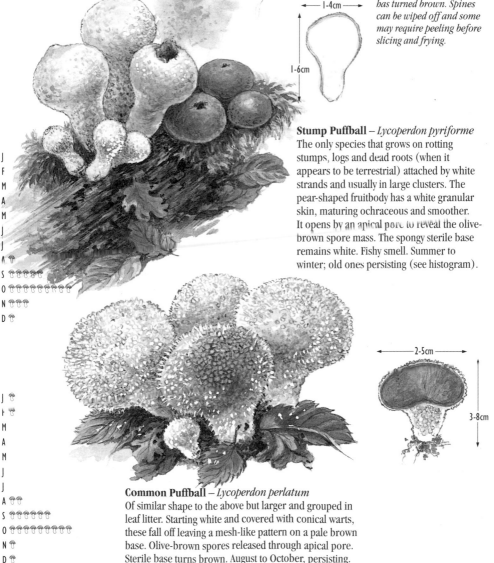

◄— 1-4cm —►

1-6cm

J
F
M
A
M
J
J
A
S
O
N
D

Stump Puffball – *Lycoperdon pyriforme*
The only species that grows on rotting stumps, logs and dead roots (when it appears to be terrestrial) attached by white strands and usually in large clusters. The pear-shaped fruitbody has a white granular skin, maturing ochraceous and smoother. It opens by an apical pore to reveal the olive-brown spore mass. The spongy sterile base remains white. Fishy smell. Summer to winter; old ones persisting (see histogram).

◄— 2-5cm —►

3-8cm

J
F
M
A
M
J
J
A
S
O
N
D

Common Puffball – *Lycoperdon perlatum*
Of similar shape to the above but larger and grouped in leaf litter. Starting white and covered with conical warts, these fall off leaving a mesh-like pattern on a pale brown base. Olive-brown spores released through apical pore. Sterile base turns brown. August to October, persisting.

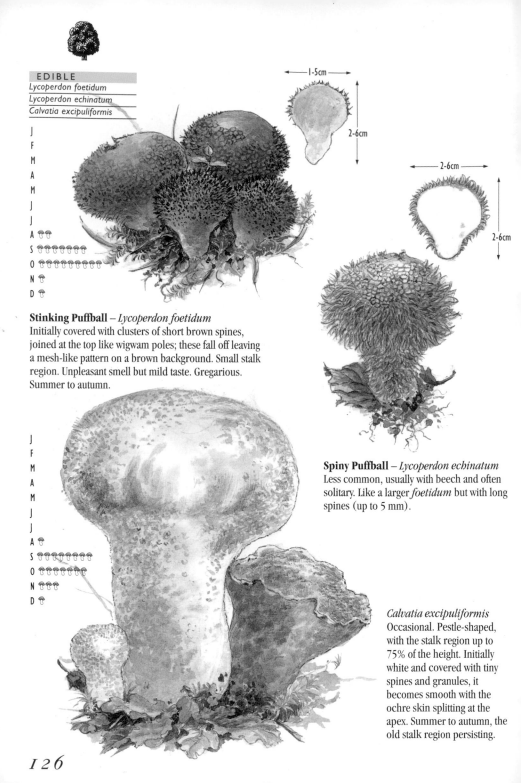

Lycoperdon foetidum
Lycoperdon echinatum
Calvatia excipuliformis

J
F
M
A
M
J
J
A
S
O
N
D

1-5cm

2-6cm

2-6cm

2-6cm

Stinking Puffball – *Lycoperdon foetidum*
Initially covered with clusters of short brown spines,
joined at the top like wigwam poles; these fall off leaving
a mesh-like pattern on a brown background. Small stalk
region. Unpleasant smell but mild taste. Gregarious.
Summer to autumn.

J
F
M
A
M
J
J
A
S
O
N
D

Spiny Puffball – *Lycoperdon echinatum*
Less common, usually with beech and often
solitary. Like a larger *foetidum* but with long
spines (up to 5 mm).

Calvatia excipuliformis
Occasional. Pestle-shaped,
with the stalk region up to
75% of the height. Initially
white and covered with tiny
spines and granules, it
becomes smooth with the
ochre skin splitting at the
apex. Summer to autumn, the
old stalk region persisting.

Lookalikes

Scleroderma verrucosum
(see p. 162)

Scleroderma citrinum –
Common Earthball (see p. 162)

The very young stages of some other fungi are white and rounded and can be mistaken for a puffball:

Amanita species
Such as the Death Cap (see p. 151) which has a white veil covering the compact, globular young fruitbody. A vertical section reveals the cap and stem. **Deadly poisonous**.

Phallus impudicus – **Stinkhorn**
The 'witch's egg' is like a pointed puffball, half buried in leaf litter. Cold and soft to the touch. When cut open a jelly layer is revealed around the immature olive spore mass and white stem. The polystyrene-like stem and sticky spore mass emerge from the 'egg' which *is* edible (rated as an aphrodisiac!) but not recommended.

Piptoporus betulinus – **Birch Bracket**
Always on birch, the older ones are like thick plates but they start like eggs. The firm, rubbery texture renders them inedible, but they were once used to sharpen cut-throat razors.

Oyster Mushroom
Pleurotus ostreatus (Jacq ex Fr.) Kummer

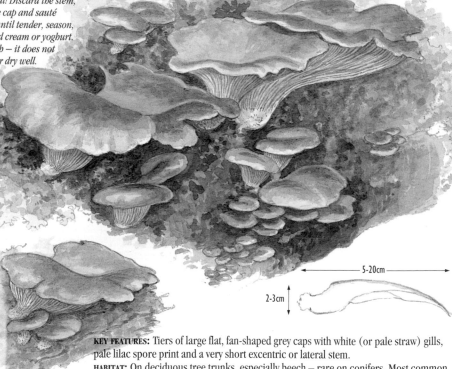

EDIBLE
Pleurotus ostreatus

COOKING AND EATING
Large caps are typically tough, maggoty and of a watery texture, so small is beautiful! Discard the stem, slice the cap and sauté slowly until tender, season, then add cream or yoghurt. Use fresh – it does not freeze or dry well.

One of the few good edible species growing on tree trunks, it is grown commercially and several varieties are now available in supermarkets. Wild ones always seem to taste better, especially when they are found on a cold January walk! None of the confusable species is poisonous.

5-20cm

2-3cm

J
F
M
A
M
J
J
A
S
O
N
D

KEY FEATURES: Tiers of large flat, fan-shaped grey caps with white (or pale straw) gills, pale lilac spore print and a very short excentric or lateral stem.

HABITAT: On deciduous tree trunks, especially beech – rare on conifers. Most common on dead wood including stumps, logs and even fence posts. The variety *columbinus* is found mostly on poplar.

FREQUENCY: Common. In dense overlapping clusters.

SEASON: Late autumn and winter (see histogram).

CAP: Very variable in colour with young caps typically slate-blue (oyster) but older ones ranging from grey through buff to almost white. Var. *columbinus* is the bluest. Fan-shaped with inrolled edges when young, smooth and moist to the touch.

GILLS: White ageing to straw, distant, decurrent and unbranched save on the stem where there are some cross-veins.

SPORE PRINT: Pale lilac (see picture). (Spores appear white under a microscope.)

STEM: Excentric, lateral or absent; tough. Downy when young. Stems often fuse, bearing caps of different ages.

FLESH: Firm, white and smelling of mushrooms. Tough near the stem which may be maggot-infested in older specimens.

WARNING: Inhalation of the spores can cause an allergy similar to 'farmers' lung'.

LOOKALIKES

There are three other common species of *Pleurotus* which have a similar habitat and growth form; *P. cornucopiae*, *P. dryinus* and *P. pulmonarius* (see pp. 130–131).

Other gill-bearing, lateral-stemmed species include:

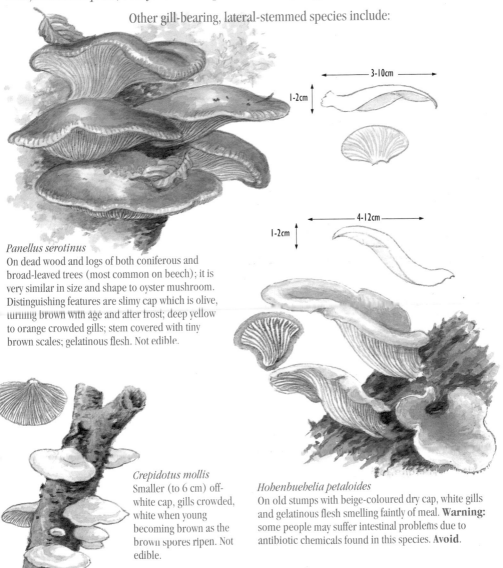

3-10cm

1-2cm

4-12cm

1-2cm

Panellus serotinus
On dead wood and logs of both coniferous and broad-leaved trees (most common on beech); it is very similar in size and shape to oyster mushroom. Distinguishing features are slimy cap which is olive, turning brown with age and after frost; deep yellow to orange crowded gills; stem covered with tiny brown scales; gelatinous flesh. Not edible.

Crepidotus mollis
Smaller (to 6 cm) off-white cap, gills crowded, white when young becoming brown as the brown spores ripen. Not edible.

Hohenbuehelia petaloides
On old stumps with beige-coloured dry cap, white gills and gelatinous flesh smelling faintly of meal. **Warning:** some people may suffer intestinal problems due to antibiotic chemicals found in this species. **Avoid**.

There are also a number of much smaller, bracket-like fungi with gills, growing on wood – **do not eat these**.

Branched Oyster Mushroom

Pleurotus cornucopiae (Paulet ex Pers.) Roll.

EDIBLE
Pleurotus cornucopiae

EDIBILITY:
As with Oyster Mushroom, discard the larger caps. Not as tasty and some find it indigestible unless well cooked.

Being mostly found on the stumps and dead standing wood of elm, it became very common following the death of the majority of our elm trees by 'Dutch elm' fungus. Much inferior as an edible species to the true Oyster Mushroom (see p. 128) with which, along with several other species, it is sometimes confused.

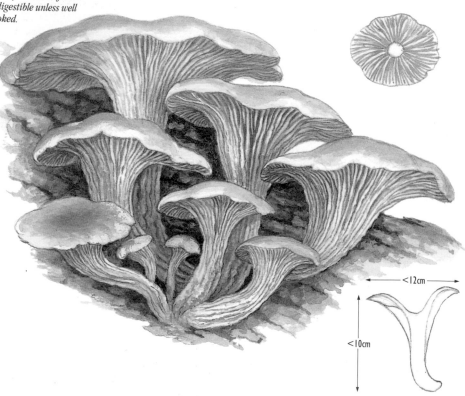

<12cm

<10cm

J
F
M
A
M
J
J
A
S
O
N
D

KEY FEATURES: Tufts of medium-sized, funnel-shaped, cream to pale brown caps. Decurrent gills forming a network over the central to slightly excentric stem.
HABITAT: On dead elm trunks and stumps, less often on beech.
FREQUENCY: Common. In dense tufts.
SEASON: Summer to early autumn; typically much earlier than Oyster Mushroom (see histogram on p. 128).
CAP: Cream to pale brown, darker at the centre, shiny, round becoming oval, flat then concave and funnel-shaped.
GILLS: Off-white, decurrent and continuing down on to the stem where they branch, forming a raised network.
SPORE PRINT: Pale lilac (see picture). Spores appear white under the microscope.
STEM: Slightly excentric, longer and more upright than in Oyster Mushroom, often fusing with others at the base. Smooth when young.
FLESH: White with an unpleasant smell.

130

Lookalikes

The most common source of confusion is with *Pleurotus ostreatus* (see p. 128). Two other *Pleurotus* species are:

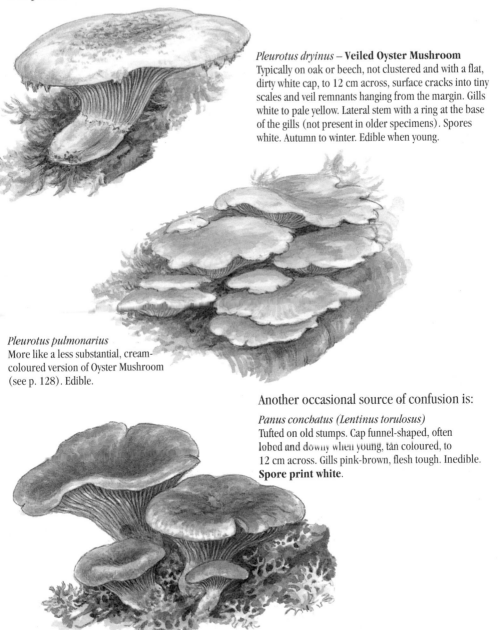

Pleurotus dryinus – **Veiled Oyster Mushroom**
Typically on oak or beech, not clustered and with a flat, dirty white cap, to 12 cm across, surface cracks into tiny scales and veil remnants hanging from the margin. Gills white to pale yellow. Lateral stem with a ring at the base of the gills (not present in older specimens). Spores white. Autumn to winter. Edible when young.

Pleurotus pulmonarius
More like a less substantial, cream-coloured version of Oyster Mushroom (see p. 128). Edible.

Another occasional source of confusion is:

Panus conchatus (Lentinus torulosus)
Tufted on old stumps. Cap funnel-shaped, often lobed and downy when young, tan coloured, to 12 cm across. Gills pink-brown, flesh tough. Inedible. **Spore print white**.

Fawn Mushroom

Pluteus cervinus (Schaeff.) Kummer

COOKING AND EATING
As with many species, maggots can be a problem but these are less likely in early or late season finds. The tender-fleshed caps are best used in stews or soups rather than on their own.

As with a number of species in this book, opinions differ as to the edibility of this fungus. Its slightly sharp flavour is not to everyone's liking but for those who enjoy the slightly nutty flavour it has a number of advantages; it is common, easily identified and has a very long fruiting season. The name *cervinus,* referring to deer, describes the colour and texture of the cap.

6-12cm

6-11cm

1-1.5cm

J
F
M
A
M
J
J
A
S
O
N
D

KEY FEATURES: Medium-sized, grey-brown to dark-brown flat cap with radiating streaks. Crowded, free gills maturing pink – as the spore colour. White stem with longitudinal brown fibrils. On rotting wood.

HABITAT: On broad-leaved stumps, fallen wood and sawdust piles.

FREQUENCY: Common but usually only in ones and twos.

SEASON: Main flush from late summer to autumn but·occurring almost throughout the year (see histogram).

CAP: Bell-shaped then flattening, sticky when wet, grey-brown with radiating streaks or darker fibrils.

GILLS: Free, thin, crowded; initially white but maturing flesh-pink.

SPORE PRINT: Salmon-pink (see picture).

STEM: Solid, white with longitudinal brown fibrils, often swollen at base.

FLESH: White, soft and smelling faintly of radish; sharp taste.

LOOKALIKES

With the exception of certain unusual (and edible) *Volvariella* species which have a volva (sack) at the stem base, the only other large fungi growing on wood with crowded, free, pink gills and pink spores are also in the genus *Pluteus*:

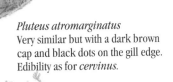

Pluteus atromarginatus
Very similar but with a dark brown cap and black dots on the gill edge. Edibility as for *cervinus*.

Pluteus umbrosus
Colour as in *cervinus* but with an irregular pattern of dark brown velvety ridges on the cap and a brown edge to the pink gills. Less common. Also edible.

A common species of similar size and with a grey-brown streaky cap, also growing on rotten wood is:

Megacollybia
(Tricholomopsis)
platyphylla
Distinguished by white, adnexed, spaced, broad gills; a white spore print and mycelial strands at the stem base. Inedible unless young.

Pluteus salicinus
Smaller, blue-grey coloured cap, similar colour at stem base; most frequent on rotten willow. Reported to contain psilocybin (see p. 20) so **best avoided**.

Brown Stew Fungus or Two-toned Pholiota

Kuehneromyes mutabilis (Schaeff. ex Fr.) Sing
(Galerina mutabilis) (Pholiota mutabilis)

COOKING AND EATING
Discard the tough stems. The caps have a strong mushroom flavour and impart a rich brown colour to soups, sauces and stews. They improve the flavour of less tasty fungi. One cluster provides a meal.

Many 'little brown jobs' with brown spores are poisonous and best avoided; this is an exception. Though small it grows in large clusters and has a very long fruiting season and, like other species growing on wood, will continue to fruit in dry weather. The common names relate to its culinary use and the changing cap colour.

←3-7cm→

3-8cm

<5mm

KEY FEATURES:
Medium-sized, tufted on dead wood. Cap smooth; centre ochraceous when dry, margin long remaining moist and date-brown. Stem pale brown above, darker and scaly below the transient ring. Crowded, adnexed pale yellow gills turning rusty-brown with the spores.

HABITAT: On stumps and fallen trunks of broad-leaved trees, especially beech.
FREQUENCY: Common, in dense tufts.
SEASON: May to December (see histogram).
CAP: Domed, becoming flat and broadly umbonate, smooth but occasionally with ribbed margins. The wet cap is uniformly date-brown and glistens. The margin retains moisture but the centre dries to a pale ochre, giving a two-tone appearance.
GILLS: Thin, crowded and adnexed. Initially pale straw, ageing rusty-brown.
SPORE PRINT: Rusty-brown (often apparent on the ring and on lower caps in a tuft).
STEM: Slender, often curved; smooth and pale brown above the transient membranous ring, dark brown and scaly below.
FLESH: Thin and straw-coloured in the cap, brown in the stem. Watery.

J
F
M
A
M 🍄🍄
J 🍄
J
A 🍄
S 🍄🍄🍄🍄
O 🍄🍄🍄🍄🍄🍄🍄🍄🍄🍄
N 🍄🍄
D 🍄

LOOKALIKES

There are several species of a similar size and colour growing in tufts on dead wood:

Flammulina velutipes – **Velvet Foot** (see p. 136)
On dead wood of broad-leaved trees, the individuals of a tuft joined at their stem bases. Distinguished by its white spores and ringless velvety stem which darkens from the yellow apex to the deep brown base. Edible.

Psathyrella hydrophila
Forming large clusters on broad-leaved tree stumps and roots, the brown caps also dry paler from the centre. Distinguished by the dark brown, adnate gills and the fragile, smooth, white, ringless stem. Spore print dark brown. Edible but bitter and not recommended.

Galerina marginata (unicolor)
In smaller clusters on dead wood and stumps **of conifers** with similar two-tone caps and brown spores but a non-scaly brown stem and a mealy smell. **Very poisonous** due to its amatoxins (see p. 18); symptoms similar to Death Cap.

Hypholoma fasciculare – **Sulphur Tuft** (see p. 163)
Distinguished by the yellow-tan caps, lack of stem scales and the purple-brown spores (appearing olive-brown on the yellow gills). Bitter tasting and **poisonous**.

Young specimens of *Armillaria mellea* – **Honey Fungus** (see picture on p. 138) can be distinguished by their stockier shape. Mature ones are much larger and have a white spore print. Edible.

Velvet Shank or *Velvet Foot*

Flammulina velutipes (Curtis) Karst. *(Collybia velutipes)*

COOKING AND EATING
Despite the velvety feel, the stems are tough and should be discarded. Wipe or peel off any remaining stickiness from the caps before cooking. Somewhat lacking in texture and flavour but providing a fresh meal in winter (they can be gathered and cooked still frozen). Much improved by the addition of a little ground, dried cep or morel.

The most unusual feature of this fungus is that it continues to fruit through the winter when the clusters of tan-yellow caps may be found adorning trunks and fallen logs. The dearth of edible species at this time accounts for its popularity, as its edible qualities are not high. A pale, cultivated form (enoki) can be bought fresh from oriental stores. There is a common poisonous species with a similar colour and habitat which also fruits in the winter.

2-8cm

3-8cm

7-10mm

J 🍄🍄🍄
F 🍄🍄
M 🍄🍄
A 🍄
M 🍄
J
J
A 🍄🍄
S 🍄🍄
O 🍄🍄🍄
N 🍄🍄
D 🍄🍄🍄🍄

KEY FEATURES: Tufts of small tan-yellow, slightly sticky caps on dark brown, velvety stems growing on dead wood. Tan gills and white spore print.

HABITAT: On trunks and fallen logs of a range of broad-leaved trees and shrubs especially elm, beech and poplar.

FREQUENCY: Common, in compact clusters of up to 30 joined by their stem bases.

SEASON: All year but peaking in the winter (see histogram).

CAP: Small, with an inrolled edge, then flat. Sticky and shiny when moist, drying matt. Colour varies from pale yellow through tan to orange-red.

GILLS: Broad, crowded, white becoming cap-coloured, adnexed.

SPORE PRINT: White (see picture).

STEM: Covered in a velvety down. Yellow at the apex, darkening to deep brown at the base. Tough, hollow, flattened and curved. Fusing with others.

FLESH: Thin, as cap colour, smell sweet.

LOOKALIKES

There are many tuft-forming species on broad-leaved wood but only the following are close enough in colour and size to cause confusion:

Hypholoma fasciculare – **Sulphur Tuft**
Common all year on stumps and logs. Tufts of sulphur-yellow caps on stems which darken towards the base. Distinguished by the presence of a ring zone and absence of velvet on the stem. Gills start yellow but mature olive-brown from the purple-brown spores. **Poisonous** and despite its bitterness it has been consumed with delayed symptoms including severe sickness. May cause liver damage.

Kuehneromyces mutabilis – **Brown Stew Fungus** (see p. 134)
Caps date-brown, drying paler in the centre, gills cinnamon, spores brown. Stem apex pale above a membranous ring, with dark brown scales below. Common on broad-leaved stumps. Edible.

Mycena inclinata
Common on oak stumps (*Flammulina* is rare on oak) with dry, smaller, bell-shaped, chestnut-brown caps, white gills and spores and a slender, smooth stem which becomes orange then brown towards the base. Inedible.

Pholiota alnicola
Occasional on broad-leaved tree stumps. The yellow-brown, greasy cap has veil remnants at the margin and yellow gills becoming rusty-brown (spore colour). Smooth stem with yellow apex, darker below the transient ring. Fruity smell. Edible but not worthwhile.

Beware the **deadly poisonous** *Galerina marginata* which grows on coniferous dead wood and is described on p. 135.

J
F
M
A
M ⚲⚲
J
J
A
S ⚲⚲⚲⚲
O ⚲⚲⚲⚲⚲⚲⚲⚲
N ⚲⚲⚲⚲
D ⚲⚲

Honey Fungus or *Bootlace Fungus*

Armillaria mellea (Vahl ex Fr.) Kummer *Armillaria mellea complex*

This common, late autumn species is so variable in its size, shape, colour and smell that accounts in different books appear to relate to separate species. Current thinking is that there are in fact three closely-related species – *A. mellea, A. bulbosa,* and *A. ostoyae* – but we will consider them together as a complex of very similar species. It is feared for its ability to infect and kill a wide range of trees and shrubs, spreading to new hosts by its thick, black bootlaces (rhizomorphs), but *A. bulbosa,* is not parasitic, being simply a rotter of dead wood. The taxonomic confusion spills over to its edibility, with some authors praising and others damning its culinary properties but all agreeing that it must be well cooked. The name *mellea* refers to the honey-coloured cap, not to a taste of honey.

5-15cm

5-12cm

1-2cm

COOKING AND EATING
Only young caps with white gills should be collected; reject stems and older caps. **Do not eat raw.** *Blanch then sauté slowly for a rich flavour and firm texture. Even after cooking it is too rich for some. Certain species may be less digestible than others (all species may be less good after freezing) so try a small amount first and then collect from the same locality. Very young ones can be pickled whole.*

KEY FEATURES: Tufts of medium-large, honey-brown caps bearing darker hairy scales at the centre when young. White veil covering young gills, later forming cottony ring on stem which springs from black 'bootlaces'. Shortly decurrent, dirty-white gills yellowing and spotting darker with age. Copious amounts of white spores.

HABITAT: *A. mellea* and *A. ostoyae* found on and around trunks and roots of living trees and shrubs (including conifers, fruit trees and privet). All three species are found on and around stumps and dead wood, including buried roots.

FREQUENCY: Common, often in large tufts.

SEASON: Late summer to early winter (see histogram).

CAP: Initially deeply convex, later flattening, even depressed and with an inrolled margin. Colour varying from honey to dark brown with olive and yellow hues. Dark brown hair-like scales present mostly near the centre on young caps.

GILLS: Obscured by yellowish white veil in young specimens (not yellow in *A. ostoyae*). Adnate to weakly decurrent, crowded, dirty-white to flesh-coloured, ageing yellower with rusty spots.

SPORE PRINT: Cream (often apparent on lower caps in a tuft and on surrounding vegetation).

STEM: *A. mellea* – densely clustered, long and slender with a large, white to yellow, cottony ring bearing yellow scales on the under side. *A. bulbosa* – less clustered, short, stocky and with a bulbous base. Transient white or yellow cobweb-like ring. *A. ostoyae* – as *bulbosa* but with a woolly ring bearing brown scales. White above the ring, olive-yellow and fibrillose near the base when young, becoming smoother and darker with age.

FLESH: Thin, soft and white. Smell ranging from none to strongly mushroomy. Bitter, soapy flavour when raw.

A. bulbosa
Shorter stocky stem with swollen base and white cottony ring.

A. ostoyae
Similar to *A. bulbosa* but ring has dark brown scales round its edge.

Pholiota squarrosa – **Shaggy Pholiota**
Size as Honey Fungus but with straw-yellow caps and lower stems covered with upturned, pointed, russet scales. Pale yellow gills becoming rusty-brown (the spore colour). On wounds of broad-leaved trees. Bitter flesh smells of radish and is not edible. **May cause reaction with alcohol** (see p. 20).

Kuehneromyces mutabilis –
Brown Stew Fungus (see p. 134)
Smaller with smooth, date-coloured caps drying paler in the centre. Thin stem with dark brown scales below the transient ring. Adnexed gills ageing rusty-brown (the spore colour). On dead wood. Edible and good.

Gymnopilus junonius
Of similar size to the Honey Fungus but of a glorious orange or tawny-brown, with fibrous scales on the cap and the adnate yellow gills becoming rusty-brown (the spore colour). The tough, bitter flesh is **poisonous**, reputedly containing psilocybin and therefore hallucinogenic.

Omphalotus olearius – **Jack O'Lantern**
In the south on sweet chestnut. Rare. The fungus is an orange colour, with a smooth cap, decurrent orange gills and a creamy-white spore print. **Poisonous**, causing severe stomach upset.

Hypholoma fasciculare – **Sulphur Tuft** (see p. 163)
Although smaller, the sulphur-yellow colour is comparable with young *Armillarias* but it is easily distinguished by the smooth cap and purple-brown spores. Flesh very bitter and **poisonous**.

Edible Bracket Fungi

Sulphur Polypore or *Chicken of the Woods*
Laetiporus sulphureus (Fr.) Murr.

This is one of the few bracket fungi that is soft enough to eat; its flavour and texture being comparable to that of chicken breast. Instantly recognisable by its colour, it is a firm favourite in North America and while many books report it as edible and good we suggest caution as it causes nausea and dizziness to a susceptible minority. It has no lookalikes.

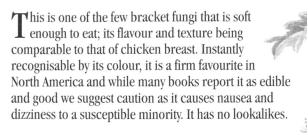

5-20cm

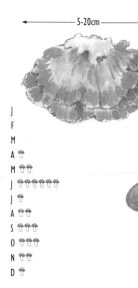

J
F
M
A 🍄
M 🍄🍄
J 🍄🍄🍄🍄🍄🍄
J 🍄🍄
A 🍄🍄🍄
S 🍄🍄🍄
O 🍄🍄🍄
N 🍄🍄
D 🍄

KEY FEATURES: Tiered clusters of thick, wavy fan-shaped brackets. Top suede-like, orange to sulphur-yellow, fading to a creamy-yellow. Undersurface of tiny, lemon-yellow pores. Succulent when young, becoming dry and brittle. White spores.

HABITAT: On a range of living trees and rotting stumps, favouring old oak, sweet chestnut, beech and yew.

FREQUENCY: Fairly common, clustered, recurring over several years.

SEASON: From early summer with some old fruit bodies persisting through the winter.

FRUITBODY: Overlapping fused clusters of lobed, fan-shaped brackets; initially succulent and with incurved folded margins and a bright orange, suede-like top; the colour becomes more sulphur and then pale yellow as it ages and dries chalky-white.

PORES: Tiny, round to oblong, yellow and exuding pale yellow droplets when fresh.

TUBES: Occupying only the bottom 5 mm of the fruitbody.

SPORE COLOUR: White.

FLESH: Thick, pale yellow and soft when young; becoming paler and more chalk-like. Strong sweet mushroomy smell and a pleasant taste (occasionally sour).

COOKING AND EATING

We must repeat that some people experience digestive and other upsets from eating this species. Some enthusiasts prefer it very young, others a little drier but old specimens are tough and indigestible. Slices can be brushed with oil and grilled or fried in breadcrumbs with lemon juice – the result being not unlike chicken. It does not dry well but will freeze (uncooked) and loses little of its flavour or texture.

COOKING AND EATING
The fruitbody absorbs tannin from the tree and very young specimens may be bitter. Do not eat when old or dry or beginning to decay. It can be eaten raw in salads but is usually sliced or cut into small pieces and stewed slowly with several changes of water to remove the tannic acid.

Beefsteak Fungus
Fistulina hepatica Schaeff. ex Fr.

The French call it the Ox-tongue, which comes closest to an accurate description of this remarkable bracket fungus. There are no confusable species, so there should be no problem with identification – the uncertainty is with its gastronomic qualities. Epithets range from the barbed 'poorman's beefsteak' (in fact this is a visual comparison and does not refer to its taste) to 'wonderful eaten raw in salads'. As ever it is a matter of personal taste. There is also considerable variation in flavour and texture.

J
F
M
A
M
J
J
A
S
O
N
D

20-40cm

KEY FEATURES: A large, thick, tongue-shaped, moist-fleshed bracket. Upper surface rounded, rough, sticky and orange-red; ageing flat, smoother, dry and red-brown. Yellow pores, bruising red-brown and exuding a blood-like juice. Tubes moist, separable from one another and the thick, streaked flesh resembling raw meat.

HABITAT: Old oak or sweet chestnut, in the lower regions of the main trunk; stumps.

FREQUENCY: Fairly common. Solitary but recurring on the same tree over several years.

SEASON: Late summer to autumn (see histogram).

FRUITBODY: Semi-circular or tongue-shaped, with little or no obvious stem. Convex above and with inflated, rounded margins; later flat with sharp edges. Soft and moist when young, becoming firm and dry. Top rough, especially at the edges, sticky and pink to brick-red, ageing smoother, dry, red or liver-brown.

PORES: Visible, round and separate (see picture). Initially cream to pale yellow but bruising and ageing red-brown and often exuding a blood-red juice.

TUBES: 1 cm long, not fused and so readily separable from each other.

SPORE COLOUR: Pinkish-yellow.

FLESH: Thick, heavy and succulent. Smell pleasant; taste mild, sometimes sour.

Dryad's Saddle or Scaly Polypore
Polyporus squamosus Fr.

The Dryad's Saddle takes its name from its supposed use by horse-riding wood-nymphs. The shape is more like an old-fashioned tractor seat.

COOKING AND EATING
Must be young, the tenderest regions being at the edges and away from the stem. Slice thinly and deep fry – overcooking makes it tough. The flavour is milder than the smell; the texture is like meat.

<50cm

KEY FEATURES: Large, fleshy, semi-circular or saddle-shaped, creamy-yellow with concentric zones of brown scales. Undersurface of pale yellow, polygonal pores. Short, black, lateral or excentric stem.

HABITAT: On a range of broad-leaved trees, especially elm, ash, sycamore and beech. On logs, stumps and living trunks.

FREQUENCY: Common, often in overlapping clusters

SEASON: Spring to summer (see histogram). Old ones persist.

FRUITBODY: Initially rounded with several flat-topped stalks – the tops expanding to large, semi-circular or fan-shaped caps. Concentric rings of brown, flat scales alternate with a tan background.

PORES: Creamy-yellow, visible, irregularly polygonal.

TUBES: 1 cm deep, extending to the stem.

SPORE COLOUR: White (see picture).

FLESH: Creamy-white, soft – becoming corky with age. Mealy smell.

J
F
M
A 🍄
M 🍄🍄🍄🍄🍄🍄🍄
J 🍄🍄🍄
J 🍄🍄
A 🍄🍄
S 🍄🍄🍄🍄
O 🍄
N 🍄
D

143

EDIBLE
Grifola frondosa

Hen of the Woods
Grifola frondosa (Dicks. ex Fr.) S.F. Gray

The Americans call it Hen of the Woods which is apt as it is tougher than the Chicken (see p. 141). Mostly found with oak.

COOKING AND EATING
When young it provides a substitute for the Cauliflower Fungus (see p. 174) but its more fibrous flesh needs slow cooking over a low heat. Cut into strips prior to cooking. Very young specimens can be cooked whole.

<35cm
<25cm

J
F
M
A
M
J
J
A
S
O
N
D

KEY FEATURES: Forms a cauliflower-like rosette of overlapping, grey-brown, thin, fan-shaped caps. Undersurface and spore colour are white.
HABITAT: At the base of living trunks and on stumps of various broad-leaved trees, especially oak.
FREQUENCY: Occasional, recurring in the same place for several years.
SEASON: Autumn (see histogram).
FRUITBODY: Bush-shaped with many grey-brown, leaf-like branches from a central stem. Each fan-shaped segment is radially furrowed, thin and wavy.
PORES: Small, round, creamy-white.
TUBES: Short (to 3 mm long).
SPORE PRINT: White (see picture).
FLESH: White, fibrous but not leathery. With a smell variously described as mealy, sweet or like hops but becoming less pleasant with age and then more like mice or old cheese! Sweet taste when young.

LOOKALIKES

The large size together with the concentric scales clearly distinguish Dryad's Saddle from all other bracket fungi. Hen of the Woods can be confused with:

Meripilus giganteus – **Giant Polypore**
Of similar form but each fan-shaped cap is wider and thicker, the top showing alternating bands of light and dark brown but lacking scales. The white pores and flesh age and bruise black. Grows to 1 m across. Common on stumps or at the base of beech (occasionally other trees). The taste and texture has been likened to beef liver but it requires very long, slow cooking and is generally regarded as inedible especially as it **causes gastric upset in some people**.

Sparassis crispa –
Cauliflower Fungus
(see p. 174)
Found at the foot of pine trees; with a more compact, creamy-brown, brittle fruitbody. Edible and excellent.

Jew's Ear

Auricularia auricula-judae (Bull. ex St Amans) Wettst.
(Hirneola auricula-judae)

COOKING AND EATING
Gather when young and moist, cut away the tough stalk region, slice thinly and stew slowly in milk or stock with plenty of seasoning for at least half an hour. Do not fry whole unless you want it to explode like popcorn! It has a seaweed-like consistency but inadequate cooking results in the 'like eating an India-rubber with bones in' problem. It can be kept dry and will reconstitute in water but is best ground to a powder to thicken and flavour soups and sauces.

'**P**atrick has been telling us about the juicy ear fungus', a child informed her brother. That name was more descriptive and less racist than the original, which is said to derive from 'Judas's ear' and the story that Judas hanged himself on an elder, the principal host of this fungus. One of the few fungi to be found throughout the year, it occurs on the dead wood of a wide range of trees and shrubs. Its close, non-British relative *A. polytricha* is available (dried) in Chinese supermarkets.

2-7cm

2-5cm

KEY FEATURES: Mature fruitbody about the size and shape of a human ear, soft, gelatinous and date-brown when moist but drying smaller, darker and hard. Attached to the substrate by a tiny stalk-like region, it assumes either a bracket or saucer-like growth form.

HABITAT: Most common on living and dead wood of elder, and also on dead wood of a range of broad-leaved trees and shrubs; not infrequent on beech and sycamore.

FREQUENCY: Very common, often gregarious.

SEASON: All year (see histogram).

FRUITBODY: Starts as a cup-shape with a smooth interior then elongates to an ear-shape, often with vein-like wrinkles inside. When moist it is thin, flabby and gelatinous. The outer/upper surface is slightly velvety and red-brown, the inner/lower surface is a shiny purple-brown. Attachment to the substrate is by a tiny stalk-like extension of the outer surface. In dry conditions the fruitbody contracts, darkens and becomes hard but rapidly reverts with rain.

SPORE PRINT: White (see picture).

FLESH: Thin, translucent, rubbery and with little smell or flavour.

J
F
M
A
M
J
J
A
S
O
N
D

LOOKALIKES

Auricularia mesenterica –
Tripe Fungus
From above looking like a small bracket fungus with its zoned, hairy, grey-brown fruitbody. The texture of the purple-brown undersurface is very like Jew's Ear, complete with vein-like wrinkles. In tiers on logs and stumps, especially elm; more common in the south. Inedible, despite its name.

Tremella foliacea – **Jelly Leaf**
Growing on dead branches of broad-leaved trees, this occasional species has the colour and wet, jelly-like texture of Jew's Ear but the fruitbody is contorted into brain-like folds. Inedible.

Pseudohydnum gelatinosum – **Jelly Tongue**
Feeling and looking very like Jew's Ear from above but with tiny, soft, white spines hanging from the under-surface and restricted to coniferous logs and stumps. Not common. Like eating gelatine, but can be glazed with a sugar and fruit mixture and served as a sweet!

Peziza species are occasionally found on dead wood, especially elm, (much commoner on the ground). Attached at the base of the cup-like fruitbody which is fragile. Inedible.

Exidia glandulosa – **Witches Butter**
Common on dead branches of broad-leaved trees, especially oak. The brown-black gelatinous fruitbodies start as little discs but become saucer-shaped or much lobed with age. Upper surface roughened. Inedible.

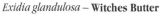

147

Poisonous Species in Broad-leaved Woodland

The Genus *Amanita*

The genus *Amanita* includes a number of fatally poisonous species; the Death Cap being the most infamous. There are over 20 species found in Britain but some are very rare and restricted to the south of England. In the following pages we describe the most important, widely-distributed species. They are not all poisonous (one non-British species, known as Caesar's mushroom is regarded as one of the best edible fungi) but we have included all the *Amanitas* together to facilitate comparison of species and because **we strongly advise against eating any** *Amanita,* where the difference between easily confusable species can be a matter of life or death.

All *Amanitas* have a universal veil which encloses the immature fruitbody (see Fig a). At maturity the veil remnants may be visible on the cap (see Fig b and *muscaria* and *pantherina*) and/or as a basal sack or volva (see Fig c and *phalloides* and *vaginata*). Not all species have a ring (see Figs d and e). They all have white spores (see Fig g), and British species all have white or cream gills, free of the stem (see Fig f). Being mycorrhizal (see p. 8), they are found associated with a range of tree species.

a. *Amanita* enclosed in veil

b. Cap with veil remnants

c. Base of stem showing volva

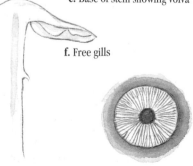

f. Free gills

d. *A. citrina* with ring

e. *A. fulva* without ring

g. White spore print

Death Cap

Amanita phalloides (Vaill. ex Fr.) Secr.

An aptly named species responsible for the great majority of deaths by fungus poisoning. The fact that it is mistaken for a Field Mushroom is at first surprising – it has an olive-green cap, white gills, a volva (though this is frequently left behind by careless picking) and is a woodland species. Ramsbottom (1953) surmised that the peelable cap skin led to the belief that it was a mushroom. One cap can kill and even the spores are poisonous so it should not be stored with edible species; but stories of poisoning from mere handling appear to be anecdotal.

TOXICITY

Contains phallotoxins and amatoxins (the latter destroyed neither by cooking nor drying) which produce no symptoms until at least five hours and up to 24 hours after ingestion. Initial symptoms include severe stomach pain, sweating, sickness and diarrhoea together with intense thirst. By this time stomach pumping or administering absorptive charcoal has limited value. The toxins break down cell membranes and are not excreted; in fact they cause kidney and liver failure, with death occurring about a week after ingestion. Modern treatment (including large doses of penicillin) has reduced the mortality rates to 20% (see p. 18).

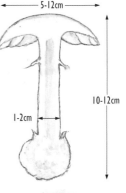

HABITAT: With broad-leaved trees, especially oak.

FREQUENCY: Occasional; much more common in southern England.

SEASON: Late summer to autumn.

CAP: Initially deeply convex and covered with a white universal veil but after expanding and flattening it rarely carries any veil remnants. Skin peelable, smooth and slightly slimy when moist, olive-yellow to greenish-bronze with darker radiating fibrils.

GILLS: Free, crowded and white – occasionally green tinted.

SPORE PRINT: White (see picture).

STEM: White with faint cap-coloured wavy zones. Becoming hollow with age. Expanded base enclosed in a white sack-like volva. Ring white and initially grooved above, pale yellow below, hanging down from the upper region of the stem.

FLESH: White, soft and sweet smelling; becoming foetid with age.

TOXICITY
*Said to contain similar
amatoxins to those in
Death Cap and produces
comparable symptoms.
Has caused many deaths.*

Destroying Angel
Amanita virosa Secr.

This fungus is as poisonous as the Death Cap but possibly more dangerous because its appearance is much closer to that of the Mushrooms (see p. 108) and in its early stages it can also be mistaken for an edible Puffball (see p. 125). Most *Amanitas* are less common in the north but *virosa* is an exception; being most frequent in Scotland.

5-10cm

5-10cm

1-1.5cm

HABITAT: With broad-leaved trees, especially birch on acid mountain soils.
FREQUENCY: Rare in England and Wales, occasional in Scotland.
SEASON: Late summer to autumn.
CAP: Initially egg-shaped and hidden in the white universal veil then expanding but remaining bell-shaped. White, smooth and slightly sticky when moist.
GILLS: Free, crowded and white.
SPORE PRINT: White (see picture).
STEM: White, slender, often curved. Bearing scales and a thin, grooved, transient ring just under the cap. Base enclosed in a white, sack-like volva.
FLESH: White and soft with a sickly sweet smell – more rank with age.

False Death Cap

Amanita citrina (Shaeff.) S.F.Gray *(Amanita mappa)*

This species is inedible (strong tasting) rather than poisonous but the yellow cap can be confused with the Death Cap while the white form (var *alba*) is more like the Destroying Angel. As these are both deadly poisonous, consumption of *citrina* should be avoided. We include it because it is far commoner than either of its more famous relatives. It can be distinguished from them by its poorly-developed volva and distinctive smell of raw potato or radish.

TOXICITY
This species is not in fact poisonous but is inedible and easily confused with poisonous species, so avoid.

HABITAT: With coniferous and broad-leaved trees, especially beech and oak.
FREQUENCY: Very common.
SEASON: Summer to autumn.
CAP: Convex but soon flattening. Pale lemon, darker at the centre; white in var *alba*. Bearing irregular (like a map) ochre-yellow veil fragments.
GILLS: Free, crowded and white with a hint of yellow.
SPORE PRINT: White (see picture).
STEM: As gill colour, grooved at the apex and with a very bulbous base; volva like a trough around the stem (not sack-like). White ring, grooved above, high up stem.
FLESH: White and with a strong smell of raw potato or radish. (We do not advise tasting even the non-poisonous *Amanitas*.)

153

Panther Cap

Amanita pantherina (DC. ex Fr.) Secr.
and *Amanita excelsa* (Fr.) Kummer *(Amanita spissa)*

The Panther Cap is very poisonous and although uncommon it is often confused with the much commoner, non-poisonous *excelsa*. So alike are the two that we describe them together – and **on no account should either species be eaten**.

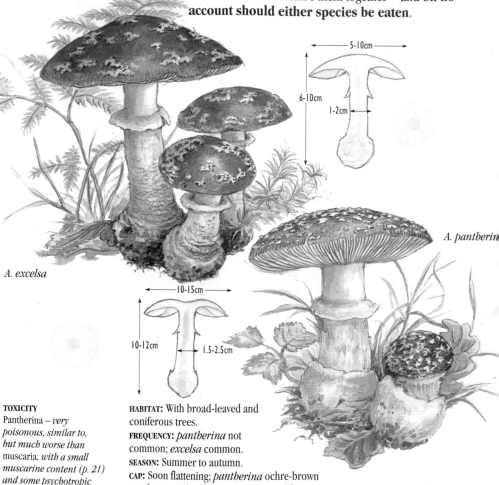

5-10cm

6-10cm

1-2cm

A. pantherin

A. excelsa

10-15cm

10-12cm

1.5-2.5cm

TOXICITY
Pantherina – *very poisonous, similar to, but much worse than* muscaria, *with a small muscarine content (p. 21) and some psychotropic chemicals.*

HABITAT: With broad-leaved and coniferous trees.
FREQUENCY: *pantherina* not common; *excelsa* common.
SEASON: Summer to autumn.
CAP: Soon flattening; *pantherina* ochre-brown evenly covered with granular white veil fragments, margin grooved; *excelsa* grey-brown with patches of pale grey veil fragments. Rain may wash away veil fragments.
GILLS: Free, crowded and white.
SPORE PRINT: White (see picture).
STEM: White with a membranous, white transient ring. In *excelsa* this is high on the stem and the upper surface is grooved. Volva represented by several concentric scaly rings above the swollen stem base which is like an egg-cup in *pantherina*.
FLESH: White. In *pantherina* smelling of raw potato or radish; *excelsa* has an earthy or turnip-like smell. Do not taste *Amanitas*.

Fly Agaric
Amanita muscaria (L. ex Fr.) Hooker

T his striking fungus has been depicted on Christmas cards (see
p. 35), in children's stories and on film (Fantasia); as a result it is
perhaps the most familiar of all fungi – even among those who have
never seen it in the flesh! The common name is associated with its
earlier use as a fly killer and is also pertinent to its hallucinogenic
properties (see p. 34). Despite its reputation it is rarely fatal to humans
but its chemical cocktail produces a range of unpleasant symptoms.
When mature it cannot be confused with any edible species in Britain
and most accidental poisoning is to children. The edible *A. caesarea*
(not British) has an orange, largely unspotted cap, yellow gills and
stem and a more sack-like volva.

POISONOUS
Amanita muscaria

TOXICITY
*Muscimol and ibotenic acid
produce hallucination and
possibly coma (see p. 34).
Muscarine may induce
sweating, running eyes,
sickness and diarrhoea
(see p. 21).*

HABITAT: Most common with birch;
also with pine and spruce.
FREQUENCY: Common, gregarious and
often in rings.
SEASON: Late summer to early winter.
CAP: Initially ball-shaped and
enclosed in a white veil. This
fragments as the cap expands and
typically forms scattered scales on the
shiny, bright red skin. The margin is grooved and the skin peelable. The scales are
easily washed off and the colour may fade to orange.
GILLS: Free, thick, crowded, white to pale straw colour.
SPORE PRINT: White (see picture).
STEM: White. Solid but later hollow. Large persistent hanging ring, grooved above and
yellowing. Swollen base with rings of white scales (volval remains) on the stem.
FLESH: Soft and white, yellow beneath the cap skin. Faint smell.

10-20cm

15-20cm

2cm

The Blusher

Amanita rubescens (Pers. ex Fr.) S.F.Gray

The most common of the *Amanitas* and also the most variable. It contains different poisons from the previously described species and these render it poisonous when raw or insufficiently cooked. It can be eaten after cooking but still upsets some people and is easily confused with more dangerous species such as *A. pantherina* (see p. 154) so it should **not** be collected for consumption.

5-15cm
1-2.5cm
7-14cm

TOXICITY
Contains haemolytic compounds (see p. 19) which cause the break up of red blood cells leading to anaemia and possible kidney problems. Symptoms are only apparent from at least four hours after ingestion. The chemicals are destroyed by heat thus explaining the poisonous nature of the raw or under-cooked fungus.

HABITAT: With both broad-leaved and coniferous trees.
FREQUENCY: Very common.
SEASON: Early summer to late autumn.
CAP: Initially rounded and covered with a dirty-white veil but soon expanding and finally flattening. The veil remnants appear flesh-coloured but may be grey or pale yellow. They cover the majority of the cap in young specimens but older ones are left with only patches or a totally smooth cap, typically rosy-brown but varying from cream to dark brown.
GILLS: Free, crowded and white but bruising pinkish-red.
SPORE PRINT: White (see picture).
STEM: Broad. Initially white but becoming increasingly flecked and bruising pinkish-brown below the white, hanging, grooved ring. Little sign of the volva on the bulbous base other than the encircling ridge.
FLESH: White but going pink on exposure, especially at the stem base where it is often maggot infected.

Grisette and *Tawny Grisette*

Amanita vaginata (Bull. ex Fr.) Vitt.
Amanita fulva (Schaeff.) Secr.
(Both previously *Amanitopsis*)

POISONOUS
Amanita vaginata
Amanita fulva

Not all *Amanitas* have a ring and the Grisette (grey clad) and the Tawny Grisette are the most common ringless species. Both are regarded as edible but as with the Blusher (see p. 156) they must be well cooked and Grisette can be confused with both the Death Cap (see p. 151) and the Panther Cap (see p. 154), both of which may lose their rings. We strongly urge against eating any *Amanita* species.

TOXICITY
The Grisettes do not contain any amatoxins but the presence of haemolytic compounds make them dangerous when eaten raw or under-cooked; symptoms as for A. rubescens *(see p. 156).*

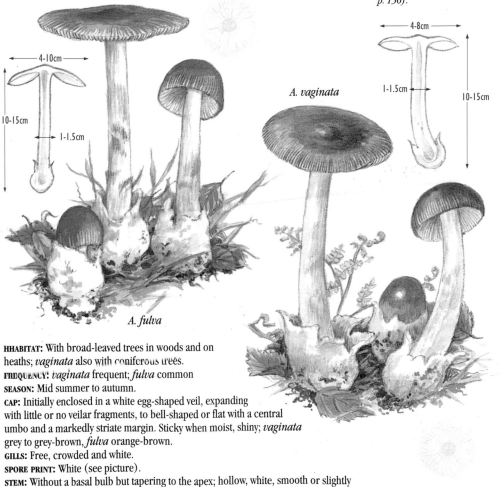

A. vaginata

A. fulva

HHABITAT: With broad-leaved trees in woods and on heaths; *vaginata* also with coniferous trees.
FREQUENCY: *vaginata* frequent; *fulva* common
SEASON: Mid summer to autumn.
CAP: Initially enclosed in a white egg-shaped veil, expanding with little or no veilar fragments, to bell-shaped or flat with a central umbo and a markedly striate margin. Sticky when moist, shiny; *vaginata* grey to grey-brown, *fulva* orange-brown.
GILLS: Free, crowded and white.
SPORE PRINT: White (see picture).
STEM: Without a basal bulb but tapering to the apex; hollow, white, smooth or slightly scaly and flushed with the respective cap colour as is the elongated, sack-like volva. Neither species has a ring.
FLESH: Thin, white, no distinctive smell.

Brown Roll-rim

Paxillus involutus (Fr.) Fr.

This is one of the larger, common woodland species and although it is unlikely to be confused with any of the well-known edible fungi we include it in the poisonous section if only because many earlier books proclaimed it as an edible species. Recent research has shown that it can be fatal, especially when consumed over many years.

TOXICITY
When raw or undercooked it can cause severe gastric upset with sickness and diarrhoea, but young specimens were thought to be safe if well-cooked and have long been eaten in Eastern Europe. No toxin has been identified but there appears to be an accumulative poison which disrupts the circulatory system of regular consumers, causing severe illness and death.

HABITAT: On the ground in broad-leaved woods and on heaths, especially with birch.
FREQUENCY: Very common.
SEASON: July to November.
CAP: Initially convex but then flat and finally depressed and funnel-shaped. Margin remaining inrolled, downy when young then grooved and pimply. Colour ranging from olive-brown to rust-brown, spotting darker where bruised. Dry or slimy, the latter at the centre in moist weather.
GILLS: Strongly decurrent, crowded, forking and re-joining near the stem apex; ochre-brown but slowly spotting dark brown on bruising. Easily detached from the flesh (like the tubes of a Bolete).
SPORE PRINT: Rusty-brown (see picture).
STEM: Firm, wider at the top, paler than the cap but readily bruising dark brown.
FLESH: Soft, moist and yellow but turning dark brown when cut or damaged. Strong fungus smell and a sour taste.

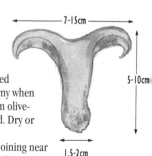

7-15cm

5-10cm

1.5-2cm

Poisonous Boletes

Devil's Bolete
Boletus satanus Lenz

Despite its name the uncommon Devil's Bolete is not fatal, but it is a serious irritant of the digestive system even when eaten in small amounts. Its reputation has spread to two other much commoner red-pored Boletes, *luridus* and *erythropus,* with many British books describing these as inedible and poisonous. By contrast Continental authors, whilst acknowledging that they must be well cooked (and even then some people find them indigestible) list them as edible. However they can be confused with *satanus* and additionally *luridus* produces alarming symptoms when consumed with alcohol. With so many good edible Boletes (see p. 92) we advise against consumption of any red-pored ones.

TOXICITY
Even small amounts cause severe sickness and diarrhoea, especially if under-cooked. Eaten in parts of central Europe after careful preparation but not recommended as edible.

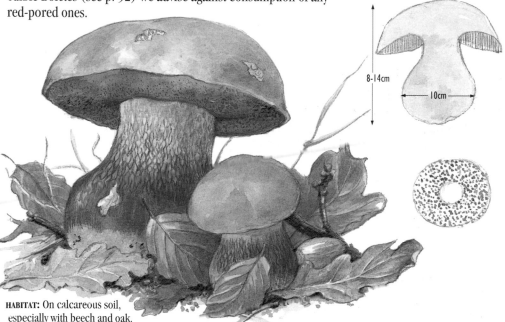

8-25cm

8-14cm

10cm

HABITAT: On calcareous soil, especially with beech and oak.
FREQUENCY: Rare, most frequent in the south. Mostly solitary.
SEASON. Late summer.
CAP: Very large, soft and slightly viscid, remaining convex with a wavy margin that extends beyond the pores. Dirty-white to olive-grey, yellowing with age.
PORES: Round, tiny, deep yellow then dark red, orange at margin, bruising blue-green.
TUBES: Orange-red, bruising blue-green.
SPORE PRINT: Olive-brown (see picture).
STEM: Solid, short and very swollen with a raised red network on a yellow background at the apex, redder below or with a red middle and paler base.
FLESH: Very thick, pale yellow – slowly bluing when cut. Unpleasant smell becoming more carrion-like with age.

Dotted-stemmed Bolete
Boletus erythropus (Fr.) Krombh.

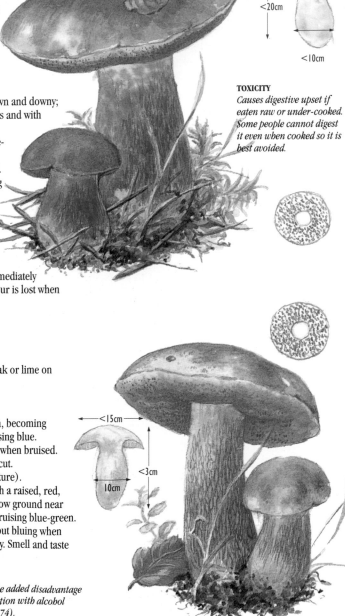

HABITAT: On the ground with both broad-leaved and coniferous trees preferring non-chalky soil.

FREQUENCY: Common. Usually solitary.

SEASON: May to November.

CAP: Large, convex, dark red-brown and downy; paler and smoother at the margins and with age. Bruising blue.

PORES: Small, round, deep orange-red; paler at the margin and with age. Rapidly bluing when bruised.

TUBES: Olive-yellow, rapidly bluing when cut.

SPORE PRINT: Olive-brown (see picture).

STEM: Thick, basically yellow but covered with orange-red dots. Bruises blue-black.

FLESH: Thick, firm and yellow, immediately turning dark blue when cut. (Colour is lost when cooked.) Little smell or taste.

TOXICITY
Causes digestive upset if eaten raw or under-cooked. Some people cannot digest it even when cooked so it is best avoided.

Lurid Bolete
Boletus luridus Fr.

HABITAT: Especially with beech, oak or lime on chalk or limestone.

FREQUENCY: Occasional.

SEASON: Summer to autumn.

CAP: Medium-sized, yellow-brown, becoming darker with age; suede-like. Bruising blue.

PORES: Orange-red, small, bluing when bruised.

TUBES: Olive-yellow, bluing when cut.

SPORE PRINT: Red-brown (see picture).

STEM: Lacking a swollen base, with a raised, red, coarse-meshed network on a yellow ground near the apex, darker near the base. Bruising blue-green.

FLESH: Thick, mostly pale yellow but bluing when cut, then fading. Becoming spongy. Smell and taste not distinctive.

TOXICITY
As for Boletus erythropus *but with the added disadvantage that it produces an unpleasant reaction with alcohol similar to the Common Ink Cap (p. 74).*

Woolly Milk Cap

Lactarius torminosus (Shaeff. ex Fr.) S.F.Gray

While the English name refers to its appearance, the Latin 'suffering from colic' describes its effects! This is a feature of some other Milk Caps but *torminosus* is the most notorious; being confused with the edible Saffron Milk Cap (p. 166). In fact its effects are more unpleasant than serious and only occur if it is eaten raw or under-cooked. In parts of northern Europe it is consumed after careful preparation – the irritant chemicals being removed by repeated changes of boiling water.

POISONOUS
Lactarius torminosus

6-12cm

6-10cm

2cm

HABITAT: On acid soil in woods and heaths, wherever birch is present.

FREQUENCY: Frequent.

SEASON: Late summer to autumn.

CAP: Soon becoming funnel-shaped, sticky at the centre when moist and with an inrolled woolly margin. Flesh-coloured with darker concentric rings. *L. pubescens* is very similar but has a creamy, non-zoned cap.

GILLS: Pink, crowded and weakly decurrent. Scratching produces a white acrid milk.

SPORE PRINT: Creamy-yellow (see picture).

STEM: Pink, smooth or with occasional pits, equal and soon becoming hollow.

FLESH: Thick, creamy and exuding lots of white milk. Smell faint, taste very acrid.

TOXICITY
The peppery taste is largely responsible for the griping pains and stomach upsets. Parboiling can remove the problem, but not recommended as an edible.

TOXICITY
Not deadly but can cause stomach ache, sickness and diarrhoea, especially when old or eaten raw.

The Earthballs

Scleroderma citrinum Pers. *(S. aurantium) (S. vulgare)* and *Scleroderma verrucosum* (Bull.) Pers.

Their outward appearance results in confusion with the edible Puffballs (see p. 125) while their habitat and internal structure is more like that of the Truffles (see p. 120) for which they have been fraudulently substituted. Earthballs have also been used to stuff sausages but they are poisonous either raw or if cooked and eaten in quantity, especially when mature.

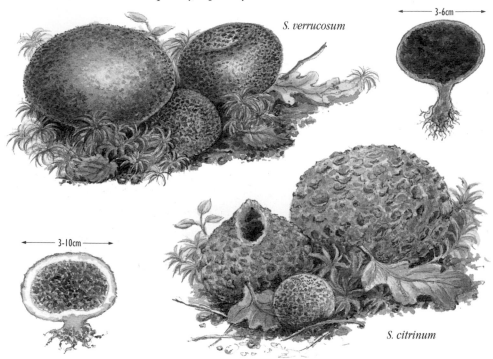

S. verrucosum

3-6cm

3-10cm

S. citrinum

HABITAT: Both species grow in woodland on acid soil, on peaty and sandy heaths and even on pavements; on, or partly buried in the soil, (or tarmac) but always associated with trees, especially birch and oak.

FREQUENCY: *Citrinum* very common, *verrucosum* frequent. Both often gregarious.

SEASON: Summer to autumn, old fruitbodies may persist through the winter.

FRUITBODY: In *citrinum,* spherical or slightly flattened, sometimes lobed, almost stalkless and with a thick (to 5 mm), yellow-brown, reptile-like scaly skin. Smell rubbery. Interior initially firm and white but soon becoming purple-black with whitish marbling and finally powdery and dark brown. Brown spores released through irregular apical splits in the skin. In *verrucosum,* more pear-shaped with a thinner skin covered in small brown scales (these can wear away) and a short, grooved stalk-like base. Smell faint. Other features similar to *citrinum.*

There are several other British species (including *S. areolatum*) but they can only be accurately identified on spore shape.

Sulphur Tuft

Hypholoma fasciculare (Hudson ex Fr.) Kummer

O ne of the commonest stump-rotting fungi, forming large tufts of yellow fruitbodies throughout the year. It is unlikely to be eaten on its own due to its very bitter taste but it has been consumed with other fungi and can be confused with three edible, tufted, stump-rotters: Velvet Shank (p. 136), Brown Stew Fungus (p. 134) and Honey Fungus (p. 138). It was formerly regarded as merely inedible but is now classed as poisonous.

◄— 3-7cm —►

5-10cm

5-10mm

HABITAT: On stumps, logs and dead roots of broad-leaved trees; more rarely on those of conifers.

FREQUENCY: Very common, gregarious; forming tufts.

SEASON: All year, most common in autumn.

CAP: Bell-shaped then flattened with a broad umbo. Margin initially incurved and with remnants of the veil. Silky, dry and a sulphur-yellow colour, fading with age and becoming more orange-tan at the centre.

GILLS: Crowded, adnate to sinuate, initially enclosed in a pale yellow veil. Changing from yellow through olive to purple-brown.

SPORE PRINT: Purple-brown (see picture).

STEM: Pale yellow at the apex, darkening to tan-brown beneath the spore-coloured ring-zone. Rarely straight. Hollow.

FLESH: Firm, yellow to brown. Iodine smell and bitter taste (like quinine).

TOXICITY
Symptoms of stomach ache and sickness do not appear until eight or nine hours after ingestion. It contains some of the Amanita *poisons which cause liver damage and has proved fatal when eaten in Japan.*

Edible Species in Coniferous Woodland

Woods containing our native Scots Pine contain many species, including some restricted to pine. Some of the introduced conifers such as Norway Spruce, especially those grown in plantations, are also good hunting grounds, but in general, broad-leaved or mixed woodlands provide a greater range of species. Species described under Edible Species in Broad-leaved Woodland that also occur in coniferous woodland include: Common Yellow Russula (p.85), Penny Bun (p.92), Bay Bolete (p.94), Deceiver (p.112), Hedgehog Fungus (p.118), woodland Puffballs (p.125) and Honey Fungus (p.138).

Saffron Milk Cap
Lactarius deliciosus (L. ex Fr.) S.F. Gray

EDIBILITY
Briefly blanch to remove any trace of bitterness then dry and fry, or better still grill, to appreciate the crisp texture. Goes well with fish and other more strongly flavoured foods.

Depicted on a 2,000-year-old Roman fresco; its Latin name denotes the culinary standing of this the most celebrated of the edible Milk Caps. Some authors are less enthusiastic, referring to its resinous flavour, but this almost certainly refers to a very similar species which was not formerly separated – see confusable species! The crisp texture and spectacular colour make the true Saffron Milk Cap a talking point at any dinner party.

J
F
M
A
M
J
J
A
S 🍄🍄🍄🍄🍄🍄🍄
O 🍄🍄🍄🍄🍄🍄🍄🍄🍄🍄🍄
N 🍄🍄
D

KEY FEATURES: Large, funnel-shaped, pale orange cap with concentric rings of deep orange spots. Short, broad, orange stem often with darker pits near the base. Bright orange gills which, when broken, exude a mild-tasting carrot-coloured milk which slowly turns green. This green staining is found in older specimens on the cap, stem and gills.

HABITAT: With pine.

FREQUENCY: Not common, but gregarious and locally frequent.

SEASON: Late summer to autumn (see histogram).

CAP: Convex, then flattening with a small central depression. Margin initially inrolled, later lobed and wavy. Skin slightly sticky, cream to pinkish-orange with concentric bands of deep orange. Slightly hoary. Later fading and with slight green staining.

GILLS: Crowded, slightly decurrent, bright orange. Scratching produces a mild-tasting, carrot-coloured milk which slowly turns dull green and stains the gills.

SPORE PRINT: Pale yellow (see picture).

STEM: Short, thick and hollow. Paler than the cap but with carrot-coloured pits near the base. Bruising green.

FLESH: Firm, pale yellow, rapidly changing to orange (from the milk) and later to green. Faint smell. Mild or slightly bitter taste.

LOOKALIKES

There are two closely related species which are most easily separated
by their different habitat:

Lactarius deterrimus
With spruce *(Picea)* (e.g. in forestry plantations). Cap
orange, smooth, greening with age and after frost. Stem
rarely pitted, paler at the apex. Gills orange as is flesh and
milk which gradually turn wine-red and finally dark green.
Cooking reduces the bitterness of the flesh but this is a
much less palatable species than *deliciosus* with which
it is frequently confused.

Lactarius salmonicolor
With fir *(Abies)*. Cap orange and flesh-coloured, no
zoning or greening. Stem sometimes pitted. Orange
milk changing reddish brown. Flesh bitter.
Edibility as above.

Two **poisonous** species are:

Lactarius helvus
On wet ground with pine or birch. The rough yellow-
brown cap is unzoned, the stem and gills are as the cap
colour. The milk is like water. Strong smell of fenugreek.

Lactarius torminosus – **Woolly Milk Cup** (see p.161)
With birch (not with conifers). Flesh-pink stem, gills and
cap; the latter with concentric darker zones similar to
deliciosus. Distinguishable by the shaggy wool-like cap
margin and the white, peppery milk.

Brown Wood Mushroom
Agaricus silvaticus Schaeff. ex Secr. *(Psalliota silvatica)*

EDIBILITY
A passable substitute for the Field Mushroom but thinner fleshed and more prone to maggot infection.

The commonest Mushroom of conifer woods but its scaly brown cap is not most people's idea of a Mushroom so it is often overlooked especially when it merges with its habitat. Despite the thin flesh and mild taste it is a good edible species.

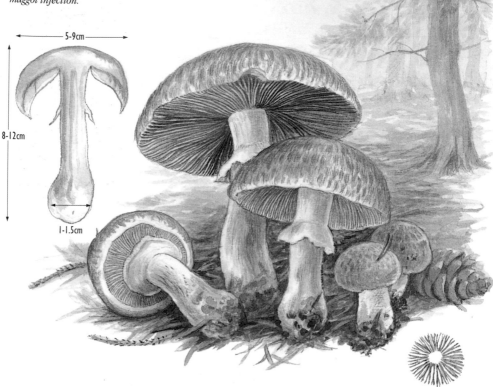

5-9cm

8-12cm

1-1.5cm

J
F
M
A
M
J
J
A 🍄🍄🍄🍄
S 🍄🍄🍄🍄🍄🍄🍄🍄
O 🍄🍄🍄🍄🍄🍄🍄🍄
N
D

KEY FEATURES: Medium-sized, pale ochre cap covered with brown fibrous scales. Thin stem with bulbous base and persistent, large ring. Gills with a reddish tinge, maturing dark brown. Cut flesh in cap and stem changing blood red. With conifers.

HABITAT: With conifers.

FREQUENCY: Fairly common. Locally abundant.

SEASON: Late summer to autumn (see histogram).

CAP: Covered with brown fibrils or scales on a pale background but very variable.

GILLS: Enclosed in a white veil and grey-pink when young. Becoming deep brown. Crowded, narrow, free.

SPORE PRINT: Very dark brown (see picture).

STEM: Long, thin, hollow, with bulbous base. Dirty white. Large, simple, pale grey ring below which the stem is somewhat scaly.

FLESH: Thin in cap. White, becoming orange-red and finally blood-red on cutting. Old specimens may become brown-fleshed and not redden. Pleasant smell and taste.

Lookalikes

Confusion is most likely with other *Agaricus* (Mushroom) species, most of which are edible and good to eat.

A. haemorrhoidarius – **Bleeding Brown Mushroom** (see p. 105) Very similar but is found with broad-leaved trees and has a stouter stem.

A. augustus –
The Prince
In grass under various trees including spruce and yew; not common. Distinguishable by its larger size (cap to 20 cm), scaly cap bruising deep yellow and margins with overhanging veil remains. Stem bruising yellow and with very large floppy ring. Thick flesh not reddening, smelling of almonds. Edible and excellent – named after the Roman emperor with whom it was a favourite.

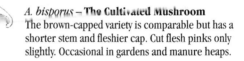

A. bisporus – **The Cultivated Mushroom**
The brown-capped variety is comparable but has a shorter stem and fleshier cap. Cut flesh pinks only slightly. Occasional in gardens and manure heaps.

A. variegans (impudicus)
With concentric rings of almost square, brown scales on a pale background, flesh in stem apex flushing slightly and with a sharp smell. Stem base bulbous. With conifers. Edible but poor.

One other group of lookalikes include:

The Parasol Mushrooms – *Macrolepiota spp*
Sometimes with coniferous trees. Distinguished by larger cap, longer stem and **white** gills. See p. 58 for edibility warning.

EDIBILITY
First remove the slimy skin. Failure to do this may result in a purgative effect. Flesh from the cap and stem is tender and usually maggot free but lacks flavour. Young ones can be dried, resulting in more flavour.

Slippery Jack

Suillus luteus (Fr.) S.F.Gray *(Boletus luteus)*

An autumn species found under conifers, normally with Scots pine. The slimy cap surface, reminiscent of slug trails, deters those looking for a meal but it is easily removed, leaving an edible, rather than excellent, fungus. Several similar species are also edible.

6-12cm

5-10cm

2-2.5cm

J
F
M
A
M
J
J
A
S
O
N
D

KEY FEATURES: Medium-sized, slimy, chestnut-brown cap. Pores small, yellow to brown, at first covered by a white veil, the remnants producing a large ring above which the stem is covered with brown dots. Under pines.

HABITAT: On the ground under Scots pine, occasionally with non-native *Pinus* species.

FREQUENCY: Fairly common especially in pine plantations. Singly or in small groups.

SEASON: Autumn (see histogram).

CAP: Chestnut-brown covered with a glutinous layer, drying shiny. Convex then flatter.

PORES: At first covered with a white membranous veil. Small, yellow, mottling brown with age.

TUBES: Pale yellow, adnate to slightly decurrent. Spongy.

SPORE PRINT: Dirty brown (see picture).

STEM: Yellow-brown below the floppy ring (white above, vinaceous beneath) pale yellow with brown granules above.

FLESH: Soft, pale yellow. No distinctive smell or taste.

LOOKALIKES

There are several other, similar-sized, *Suillus* species (with sticky caps) which are found with pine. All are edible after careful removal of the glutinous cap skin.

S. flavidus
Yellow cap, among *Sphagnum* (bog moss) in Scotland.

S. granulatus
Orange cap, stem with white granules but no ring, both stem and pores weeping milky droplets

S. variegatus
Tawny, slightly scaly, less sticky cap, tan coloured, ringless stem, strong mouldy smell.

S. bovinus
The colour of oxen (or Jersey cows), pores large, some subdivided, tubes decurrent, no ring.

Leccinum scabrum – **Brown Birch Bolete** (see p. 98) is similar from above but it has a dry cap, scaly stem, lacks a ring and grows with birch. Edible.

Two other lookalikes are found with different trees:

Suillus grevillei – **Larch Bolete** (see p. 172) has a slimy, yellow cap and grows with larch. Edible.

Brown-capped species of *Boletus* (see p. 92) have dry caps and lack the ring.

Larch Bolete

Suillus grevillei (Klotsch) Sing. *(Boletus elegans)*

EDIBLE
Suillus grevillei

COOKING AND EATING
Remove the slimy cap skin (and the tubes in older specimens) to prevent gastric upsets. Best for soups and stews. Drying increases the flavour.

This common fungus is always found on the ground near larch. Its bright yellow colour makes it easy to spot especially when growing in grass. Like its close relative the Slippery Jack (see p. 170), the slimy cap surface must be removed prior to cooking.

4-12cm

5-10cm

1.5-2cm

J
F
M
A
M
J 🍄🍄
J 🍄
A 🍄🍄🍄🍄🍄
S 🍄🍄🍄🍄🍄🍄🍄🍄
O 🍄🍄🍄
N 🍄
D

KEY FEATURES: Medium-sized, slimy, golden-yellow cap. Yellow pores, bruising brown, initially covered by a pale yellow veil, the remnants producing a transient ring above which the stem is faintly netted. Under larch.

HABITAT: On the ground with larch.

FREQUENCY: Common. Often in rings.

SEASON: Summer to late autumn (see histogram).

CAP: Domed and orange, becoming flatter and golden yellow. Covered with a glutinous layer, drying shiny.

PORES: At first covered with a pale yellow, membranous veil. Becoming angular, sulphur-yellow and bruising rusty-brown.

TUBES: Yellow, adnate to slightly decurrent. Spongy.

SPORE PRINT: Yellow-brown (see picture).

STEM: Yellow with rusty streaks below the pale, floppy ring which is coloured by the spores and soon disappears leaving a light coloured zone. Above this the yellow stem bears granules or a faint network.

FLESH: Pale yellow, flushing lilac in the cap, blue in the stem base. Mild taste.

LOOKALIKES

There are two other edible but uncommon *Suillus* species (with sticky caps and a ring) also found with larch:

S. aeruginascens (laricinus)
(was *Boletus viscidus*)
Has a wrinkled grey-yellow cap. Grey pores bruise green.

S. tridentinus
With a less sticky, orange cap and mostly compound, orange pores; mainly in the south.

Two other lookalikes can be distinguished by their habitat:

Leccinum versipelle –
Orange Birch Bolete
(see p. 96)
This is a similar colour when viewed from above, but has a larger dry cap, a scaly stem lacking a ring and is restricted to birch woods. Edible.

Suillus luteus – **Slippery Jack** (see p. 170)
Has a brown sticky cap and grows with pine. Edible.

Orange-brown species of *Boletus* (see p. 92) lack the ring and slimy cap.

Cauliflower or *Brain Fungus*
Sparassis crispa Wulf. ex Fr.

COOKING AND EATING
Do not gather when brown; it will be tough, bitter and could cause digestive upset. Carefully cut away regions that are very dirty and shake out loose material before heading for home. Cut into chunks to aid cleaning – its texture allows a thorough washing to remove the pine needles and sheltering creatures. Delicious baked or fried with butter, parsley and seasoning or try deep frying in batter. A good flavour addition to soups and stews, it dries and reconstitutes well – useful if you find a big one!

Few who have eaten it would omit the Cauliflower Fungus from their 'Top 20' best edible fungi. Its unusual form, large size and very restricted habitat should make it easy to recognise; but in their eagerness to experience this culinary feast, collectors have consumed other species – mostly those associated with broad-leaved trees.

←— 15-40cm —→

10-20cm

J
F
M
A
M
J
J
A
S
O
N
D

KEY FEATURES: The size, shape and appearance of a cauliflower heart or natural sponge, with no distinct cap, stem or gills but a mass of convoluted, flattened branches; initially cream-coloured with pale yellow tips, becoming brown all over. With pine.

HABITAT: A root parasite of pine and found on or near pine stumps or more typically on the ground beside living pine trunks. Occasionally with other conifers.

FREQUENCY: Occasional, usually solitary and recurring at the same site for many years.

SEASON: Late summer to autumn (but see p. 11) (see histogram).

FRUITBODY: With the appearance and size of a natural sponge. Spore bearing tissue in the form of much branched, flattened, leaf-like lobes; twisted and brain-like. Easily broken when young. Cream with pale yellow tips, ageing brown. The fleshy stem is often buried and root-like.

SPORE PRINT: Creamy-yellow.

FLESH: Thin, white and brittle but tougher with age and near the stem. Smell pleasant, taste similar to hazel nut.

LOOKALIKES

There are two rare *Sparassis* species: *S. laminosa* with oak or beech is much less branched. *S. simplex* on pine litter has only one flat lobe. For conservation reasons and the fact that their flesh is tough we do not advise collecting these species.

Ramaria botrytis
A rare species in beech litter about half the size of *Sparassis* with an undivided basal region, rounded, cream-coloured branches with deep-red tips and looking more like a coral. Edible but bitter at the tips and older specimens are confusable with *R. formosa* which also grows with beech but has pink branches with yellow tips. **A violent purgative**; so not recommended!

There are a number of much smaller coral fungi which are common in both coniferous and broad leaved woods e.g.

Clavulina cristata
Looking like a white, branching coral but soft, brittle and pleasant smelling. *C. cinerea* is separated by its grey-brown colour. Both are edible but insubstantial and not recommended.

Another cauliflower-like fungus is:

Grifola frondosa – **Hen of the Woods**
(see p. 144)
Also has a cauliflower-like form but the horizontal, overlapping grey-brown lobes have pores on their under-surface. Grows at the base of living trunks and on stumps of broad-leaved trees, especially oak. Edible when very young.

Poisonous Species in Coniferous Woodland

Species described under Poisonous Species in Broad-leaved Woodland that also occur in coniferous woodland include: False Death Cap (p. 153), Panther Cap (p. 154), Fly Agaric (p. 155), Blusher (p. 156) and Dotted-stemmed Bolete (p. 160).

False Chanterelle

Hygrophoropsis aurantiaca (Fr.) Maire

T his species is frequently consumed in mistake for the true
Chanterelle (p. 114). Most books list it as edible though its thin
texture and lack of flavour make it hardly worthwhile. There are
however reports that some people suffer digestive upsets and
hallucinations following its consumption, especially when under-
cooked. It is related to the poisonous Brown Roll-rim (p. 158) and
our advice is to seek out the real Chanterelle and ignore this one.

POISONOUS
Hygrophoropsis aurantiaca

TOXICITY
*Diarrhoea, sickness and
hallucinations reported
in a small percentage
of consumers. Toxic
compound unknown.*

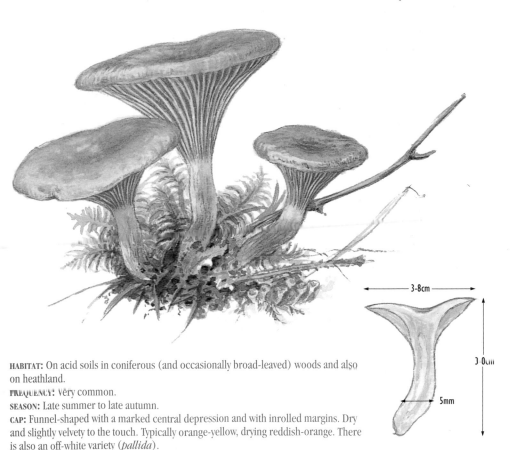

3-8cm

5mm

HABITAT: On acid soils in coniferous (and occasionally broad-leaved) woods and also
on heathland.

FREQUENCY: Very common.

SEASON: Late summer to late autumn.

CAP: Funnel-shaped with a marked central depression and with inrolled margins. Dry
and slightly velvety to the touch. Typically orange-yellow, drying reddish-orange. There
is also an off-white variety (*pallida*).

GILLS: Decurrent, crowded, thin. Forking but not reuniting. Concolorous with cap.

SPORE PRINT: White (see picture).

STEM: Sometimes slightly excentric and often curved. Slender and tapering to the base.
Becoming hollow. As cap colour or darker.

FLESH: Thin, yellow, soft but tough. No distinctive smell or taste.

The Sickener and The Beechwood Sickener

Russula emetica (Schaeff. ex Fr.) S.F.Gray
and *Russula mairei* Sing.

There are a number of cherry-red Russulas and older books conveniently separate the two commonest mainly by habitat – *R. emetica* with pine and *R. mairei* with beech. Recently taxonomists have described a larger group of species and varieties, all with an acrid taste which causes digestive upsets alluded to in the common names.

R. mairei

R. emetica

TOXICITY

Sickness and diarrhoea results if either species is eaten raw or fried. The toxic chemicals are heat-sensitive and, as with some other poisonous species, the Sickeners are edible (being consumed in N. Europe) after parboiling and careful preparation, but we cannot recommend them.

HABITAT: *emetica* with pine or birch, (occasionally with other broad-leaved trees) on acid soil, often with *Sphagnum* (Bog moss); *mairei* with beech.

FREQUENCY: Common.

SEASON: Late summer to autumn; *emetica* starting earlier.

CAP: *emetica* fragile (crumbly), shiny, scarlet to blood-red (occasionally with paler patches), 5–10 cm diameter; *mairei* firm, matt, pink to scarlet (occasionally almost white), 3–7 cm diameter. Both show pink flesh below the skin (more easily peeled in *emetica*).

GILLS: *emetica* moderately spaced, creamy-white; *mairei* – fairly crowded, white with a grey-green tint.

SPORE PRINT: White (see picture).

STEM: *emetica* spongy, white, swollen at the base; *mairei* solid, white, yellowing at the base.

FLESH: White (pink just below the skin), taste acrid, *emetica* smells fruity; *mairei* smells of coconut when young, honey when old.

Classification of Larger Fungi

CLASSIFICATION IS ONE OF THE WAYS in which humans try to make sense of relatively complex information. We try to break down the whole set into smaller sub-groups which we can order and understand more easily. We can do this using any criteria we choose; for example, in this book we have divided fungi into groups on the basis of their edibility and of their habitat. This is often called a functional classification because its sole purpose is to be useful.

Most biologists accept that the organisms that we see today have evolved by a process of natural selection over very long periods of time. Sometimes the ancestors of present-day organisms have been preserved as fossils, so we have a good idea of the changes that have taken place during their evolution. But fossilisation is a rare and chancy process, so that for most organisms we have very little fossil evidence of their ancestors. However it is possible to use the structure and biochemistry of living organisms as evidence of their relatedness. 'Natural' classifications try to group organisms so that the classification reflects our ideas about their evolution. Ideally the biologist bases the classification upon characters which are believed to be good indicators of evolutionary relatedness. In reality biologists often disagree about the relative importance of characters upon which to classify – in the case of fungi, spore colour, structure of the spore wall, biochemical features, etc. – so that they develop different ways of classifying the same group of organisms. This may seem confusing at first, but we might compare it with the attempts of several different people to reconstruct a picture from jigsaw pieces, many of which are missing and whose box has been lost. As we learn more about the fungi, or find more of the pieces, so there will be less variation between attempts by different people.

The basic unit of biological classification is the species, composed of individuals that can breed with each other and which share a large number of common features. Similar species are grouped together in a genus, all of whose members share certain key characters. Sometimes it can be difficult to recognise a boundary between two similar species which some biologists would combine into one larger, more variable species – taxonomists can themselves be classified functionally into 'splitters' and 'lumpers' by their attitude to this problem! Similar genera are grouped into families, families into orders and orders into divisions of the fungal kingdom. Needless to say, there are many different views on just how these groupings should be made. For example the agarics (mushrooms and toadstools) have all been united into one order, the Agaricales, by Singer, whereas Kuhner has divided them into five. Other classifications fall somewhere between these two extremes. Our experience is that the five-order system of Kuhner provides a straight-forward and workable one that our students have found useful and the following synopsis is based on his scheme. We have not attempted to include the full range of genera, but have concentrated on those dealt with in this book.

Kingdom Mycota

The fungal kingdom can be divided into two Divisions, the Myxomycota (slime moulds and their allies) and the Eumycota (true fungi).

Division Eumycota

All the fungi which produce large fruitbodies belong to two Subdivisions of the Eumycota, the Basidiomycotina and the Ascomycotina.

Subdivision Basidiomycotina (basidiomycetes)

Basidiomycetous fungi produce their sexual spores (basidiospores) on the tips of fine projections (sterigmata) from specialised cells called basidia. Basidia are usually arranged into a fertile layer (hymenium) borne on a fruitbody (basidiocarp).

The Basidiomycotina can be separated into several classes by the kind of basidium and by the arrangement of the hymenium. We are concerned with two of these.

CLASS HYMENOMYCETES
The hymenium forms a fertile layer over the surface of the fruitbody; the basidia discharge their spores actively from the hymenium. Usually the spores are then carried away by air currents.

Order Cantharellales – 'chanterelles' and their allies
Fruitbody fleshy and either funnel-shaped or mushroom-shaped. No true gills; the hymenium is either smooth or on radiating ridges on the underside of the fruitbody.
Family Cantharellaceae. Always mycorrhizal.
Cantharellus, Craterellus

Order Boletales – 'boletes' and their allies
Fruitbody fleshy and mushroom-shaped. The hymenium lines tubes or covers gills on the underside of the cap.
Family Boletaceae
Hymenium lines spongy tubes. Spores brown, pink or black. Always mycorrhizal.
Boletus, Leccinum, Suillus, Tylopilus
Family Paxillaceae
Hymenium on gills. Spores brown or white.
Paxillus, Hygrophoropsis

Order Pluteales – 'pink-spored toadstools'
Fruitbody fleshy and mushroom-shaped with gills. Spores pink.
Family Pluteaceae
Gills free from stem. Spores smooth and ellipsoid. Never mycorrhizal.
Pluteus, Volvariella
Family Entolomataceae
Gills never free from stem. Spores angular.
Entoloma, Leptonia, Nolanea

Order Agaricales – 'dark-spored toadstools'
Fruitbody fleshy and mushroom-shaped with gills. Spores are usually dark coloured, often with a germ-pore (thinner area of spore wall).
Family Agaricacaceae
Spores very dark brown. Gills free from stem. Never mycorrhizal.
Agaricus
Family Coprinaceae
Spores black. Never mycorrhizal.
Coprinus, Lacrymaria, Psathyrella
Family Strophariaceae
Spores dark purple-brown. Never mycorrhizal.
Hypholoma, Psilocybe, Stropharia
Family Bolbitiaceae
Spores brown, cap surface appears to be made up of rounded cells ('cellular') under the microscope. Never mycorrhizal.
Agrocybe
Families Cortinariaceae and Crepidotaceae
Spores brown, cap surface made up of elongated cells ('filamentous') under the microscope.
Cortinarius, Crepidotus, Galerina, Hebeloma, Inocybe, Pholiota
Family Lepiotaceae
Spores white. Gills free from stem. Never mycorrhizal.
Lepiota, Leucoagaricus, Macrolepiota

Order Tricholomatales – 'white-spored toadstools'
Fruitbody fleshy and mushroom-shaped with gills. Spores white or pale, never with a germ pore.
Family Amanitaceae
Young fruitbody enclosed within universal veil. Gills free from stem. Mycorrhizal.
Amanita
Family Hygrophoraceae
Gills thick due to long basidia.
Hygocybe
Family Pleurotaceae
Fruitbody usually tough or leathery, stem often lateral or absent; decurrent gills. Growing on wood.
Pleurotus
Family Tricholomataceae
Armillaria, Calocybe, Clitocybe, Collybia, Flammulina, Hohenbuehelia, Laccaria, Lepista, Marasmius, Mycena, Omphalotus, Panellus

Order Russulales – 'cheese-caps & milk-caps'

Fruitbody fleshy and mushroom-shaped with gills. Flesh of crumbly texture due to its construction from a mixture of filamentous hyphae and pockets of rounded cells. Spores pale, decorated with warts & ridges that stain black in iodine.

Family Russulaceae
Lactarius, Russula

Order Clavariales – 'fairy clubs, coral fungi and cauliflower fungi'

Hymenium borne on the surface of an erect fruitbody.

Families Clavariaceae & Clavulinaceae
Fruitbody an erect unbranched club or a branched, coral-like shape. Hymenium covers the entire surface. Spores white.
Clavulina
Family Sparassidaceae
Fruitbody cauliflower-like, branches bearing hymenium on lower surface.
Sparassis
Family Ramariaceae
Fruitbody branched, coral-like. Spores brown.
Ramaria

Order Hericiales – 'hedgehog fungi'

Fruitbody with pendant spines bearing the hymenium.

Family Hydnaceae
Fruitbody fleshy and basically mushroom-shaped, but with spines instead of gills. Mycorrhizal.
Hydnum

Order Poriales – 'bracket fungi'

Fruitbody shelf- or bracket-shaped with pores on the lower surface which are lined by hymenium. Growing on wood.

Family Fistulinaceae
Pores can be separated from each other.
Fistulina
Family Coriolaceae
Pores cannot be separated. Fruitbody unstalked.
Grifola, Laetiporus, Meripilus, Piptoporus

Family Polyporaceae
Pores cannot be separated. Fruitbody distinctly stalked.
Polyporus

Orders Auriculariales, Dacrymycetales and Tremellales – 'jelly fungi'

Fruitbody gelatinous with distinctive basidia (septate or shaped like tuning-forks).
Auricularia, Exidia, Tremella

CLASS GASTEROMYCETES – 'stomach fungi'

At maturity the hymenium is enclosed within the fruitbody and basidiospores are retained there until released in some way.

Order Lycoperdales – 'puffballs and earth-stars'

Fruitbody sac-like, thin-walled. Wall eventually opens to release spores, usually by 'puffing'.

Family Lycoperdaceae – 'puffballs'
Fruitbody wall not splitting into layers.
Bovista, Calvatia, Langermannia, Lycoperdon, Vascellum
Family Geastraceae – 'earthstars'
Fruitbody wall multilayered, outer layer splits and peels back.
Geastrum

Order Phallales – 'stink horns' and their allies

Fruitbody wall burst open by expanding tissue within. Exposed spores dispersed by insects.

Family Phallaceae
Spore mass borne on tip of erect stalk.
Phallus

Subdivision Ascomycotina (ascomycetes)

Ascomycetous fungi produce their sexual spores (ascospores) within a sac-like cell, the ascus. A few of them bear their asci on or in a large fruit-body (ascocarp).

Order Pezizales

Fruitbodies develop either above or below ground.

Above ground fruitbodies are roughly disc-like, either with or without a stalk; their asci release their ascospores through a pore formed by the opening of an apical lid (operculum).
Subterranean fruitbodies are tuber-like; their asci do not release their spores.

Family Morchellaceae
Fruitbody stalked, fertile part usually ridged. Ascospores smooth, without oil drops.
Gyromitra, Mitrophora, Morchella
Family Helvellaceae
Fruitbody stalked, saddle-shaped. Ascospores smooth with oil-drops.
Helvella
Families Tuberaceae and Terfeziaceae
Subterranean potato-like fruitbodies (truffles). Asci persist intact. Mycorrhizal.
Choiromyces, Tuber

Order Elaphomycetales
Subterranean fruitbodies (truffles). Asci are globose and disintegrate quickly within the fruit-body. Mycorrhizal.
Elaphomycetaceae
Elaphomyces

Order Clavicipitales
Mostly parasitic upon plants and insects.
Family Clavicipitaceae
Long narrow multiseptate ascospores are discharged via a narrow pore through the thick cap of the ascus.
Claviceps

Identification Guides

A. BOOKS FOR BEGINNERS

The last 20 years has seen a proliferation of illustrated guides to fungi based largely on macroscopic characters. When chosing a book look out for the following points:

1) The number of species described and/or illustrated

There are over 3,000 species of larger fungi in the British Isles and a keen amateur could soon encounter upto 800 of these. This reduces the value of books covering only a few hundred species unless these have been carefully selected as the most common and are aimed at the total beginner.

2) The geographic region covered

Some books include species which are restricted to mainland Europe and are not found in Britain. This is acceptable in addition to a good cover of British species but not where common British species are excluded.

3) The illustrations

The choice is between colour photographs or watercolour paintings. Many beginners prefer the look of photographs but later realise that a good artist can portray fine detail and variation that is only shown by first-rate photography. The important factors include depicting all stages of the fruitbody, common variations in colour and shape, background habitat and the essential features which avoid confusion with similar-looking species. The printing quality and size of individual illustrations are also important – over-bright colours or tiny pictures only confuse.

4) The text

Are the Latin names up to date? Are older names listed? Is a common name provided? (Most beginners prefer these). Is there a sensible order to the book – either by families or by habitat (Total beginners may find the latter more acceptable). Is there a simple key which will narrow the choice down to a particular group of fungi and reduce the need to flip through the whole book to find a picture that fits? Is the text full of scientific terms and if so is there a good glossary? Does the text agree with the illustration and augment it with details of fruiting season, frequency, size, smell, texture and taste, together with spore print colour?

5) The Index

Does it list both Latin and common names? Are both genera (preferably in bold) and species names listed?

Among the many books available, we recommend:

Phillips, R. (1981) *Mushrooms and other Fungi of Great Britain and Europe*. Pan Books, London
Over 900 species described and excellent photographs showing developmental stages.

Bon, M. (1987) *The Mushrooms and Toadstools of Britain and North Western Europe*. Hodder and Stoughton, London
1500 species are described together with extensive keys. Illustrations mostly show only a single specimen.

Courtecuisse, R. and Duhem, B. (1995) *Mushrooms & Toadstools of Britain & Europe*. HarperCollins, London
3500 species described with half of these illustrated. Also contains extensive keys.

Pegler, D. (1990) *Field Guide to the Mushrooms and Toadstools of Britain and Europe*. Kingfisher Books, London
Covers about 450 of the more common species in ten colour-coded sections. Excellent text; illustrations rather bright.

Garnweidner, E. (1994) *Mushrooms and Toadstools of Britain & Europe*. HarperCollins, London.
Over 400 of the more common species photographed in habitat and arranged in six colour-coded sections.

Buczacki, S.T. (1993) *Collins Guide to the Mushrooms and Toadstools of Britain and Europe*. HarperCollins, London
A book about fungi as well as an identification book. A wide range of species included with excellent text but the small size of the illustrations is a drawback.

Buczacki, S. (1982) *Gem Guide Mushrooms and Toadstools*; Harding C.P. (1995) *Gem Photoguide Mushrooms and Toadstools*. HarperCollins, London
Two pocket-sized books describing over 200 of the mote common species likely to be found by a beginner.

B. MORE ADVANCED BOOKS

1. Books on identification

Breitenbach, J. and Kranzlin F. (1984 onwards) *Fungi of Switzerland*. Verlag Mycologia, Lucerne
Three volumes are already in print. Despite being relatively expensive and not being devoted to British species, the superb photographs (taken in the field), together with drawings of microscopic detail, and a text which discusses nomenclature changes and taxonomic information, makes this a must for the dedicated mycologist.

Moser, M. (1983) *Keys to Agarics and Boleti (Polyporales, Boletales, Agaricales, Russulales)*. English Edition. Roger Phillips, London
Lacking illustrations but with extensive keys and precise descriptions of species. An invaluable work of reference.

Henderson, D.M., Orton, P.D. and Watling, R. (1969 onwards) *British Fungus Flora: Agarics and Boleti*. Royal Botanic Gardens, Edinburgh
This ongoing series of monographs currently stands at seven volumes, each providing detailed information about a particular family or group of genera. There is also an introductory volume (out of print) with keys to families and genera. Illustrated by line drawings.
Rayner, R.W. (1968–70) *Keys to the British Species of Russula*. British Mycological Society
Contains a great deal of useful information about this very important group of fungi.

Pegler, D.N., Spooner, B.M. and Young, T.W.K. (1993) *British Truffles: A Revision of British Hypogeous Fungi*. Royal Botanic Gardens, Kew, London
This is an excellent modern account of British Truffles illustrated with line drawings, colour paintings and electron micrographs. Strongly recommended for those with a specialist interest in this group.

2. Books about Edible Fungi

Carluccio, A. (1989) *A Passion for Mushrooms*. Pavillion Books, London
A beautifully-produced book with lots of mouth-watering recipes and tips for preserving fungi. Describes some 25 edible species with photographs from Roger Phillips.

Fischer, D.W. and Bessette A.E. (1992) *Edible Wild Mushrooms of North America (A Field to Kitchen Guide)*. University of Texas Press, Austin, Texas
This book covers a much larger number of edible fungi (most of which are found in Britain) and gives good advice on possible confusable species and some very different recipes.

THE BRITISH MYCOLOGICAL SOCIETY

Organises field meetings and identification work-shops. Publishes *The Mycologist* four times a year with interesting articles about fungi. Details can be obtained by writing to: PO Box 30, Stourbridge, West Midlands DY9 9PZ.

REFERENCES MENTIONED IN THE TEXT

Allegro, J. (1970) *The Sacred Mushroom and the Cross*. Doubleday, London
Baker, T. (1989) *Origins of the word "Mushroom"*. The Mycologist 3(2): 88–90
Baker, T. (1990) *The Word "Toadstool" in Britain*. The Mycologist 4(1):25–29

Carluccio, A. (1989) *A Passion for Mushrooms*. Pavillion Books, London

Cooke, M.C. (1862) *A Plain and Easy Account of British Fungi*. Robert Hardwicke, London

Cooke, R.C. (1977) *Fungi Man and his Environment*. Longman, London, New York

Crisan, E.V. and Sands, A. (1978) *In Cultivation of Edible Mushrooms* Ed. Chang and Hayes. Academic Press

Gerard, J. (1597) *The Herball or Generall Historie of Plants*. London

Grigson, J. (1975) *The Mushroom Feast*. Penguin, London

HMSO (1940 edition) *Edible and Poisonous Fungi*. London

Heim, R. (1963) *Les Champignons toxiques et Hallucinogenes*. N. Boubee & Cie, Paris

Ing, B. (1992) *A Provisional Red Data List of British Fungi*. The Mycologist 6(3): 124–128

Keys, J.D. (1976) *Chinese Herbs – Their Botany, Chemistry and Pharmacodynamics*. Charles E. Tuttle

Legg, A. (1990) *Your Top Twenty Fungi The Final List*. The Mycologist 4(1):23–24

Matossian, M.K. (1989) *Poisons of the Past. Molds, Epidemics and History*. Yale University Press

Morgan, A. (1987) *Who Put the Toad in Toadstool?* New Scientist 25 Dec/1 Jan 44–47

Morris, B. (1988) *The Folk Classification of Fungi*. The Mycologist 2(1):8–10

Oldridge, S.G., Pegler, D.N. and Spooner, B.M. (1989) *Wild Mushrooms and Toadstool Poisoning*. Royal Botanical Gardens, Kew, London

Rai, B.K., Ayachi, S.S. and Rai, A. (1993) *A Note on Ethno-Myco-Medicines from Central India*. The Mycologist 7(4):192–193

Roser, B. and Colaco, C. (1993) *A Sweeter Way to Fresher Food*. New Scientist 15 May 24–28

Smith, M.L., Bruhn, J.N. and Anderson, J.B. (1992) *The Fungus Armillaria bulbosa is Among the Largest Living Organisms*. Nature vol 356:428–431

Taylor, R. (1980) *Who is Santa Claus?* Sunday Times 21 December 1980

Wainwright, M., Rally, L. and Ali T.A. (1992) *The Scientific Basis of Mould Therapy*. The Mycologist 6(3): 108–110

Wasson, R.G. (1967) *Soma, Divine Mushroom of Immortality*. Harcourt Brace Jovanovich, New York, London

Wasson, R.G., Ruck, C.A. and Hofmann, A. (1978) *The Road to Eleusis: Unveiling the Secrets of the Mysteries*. Harcourt Brace Jovanovich, New York, London

Glossary

N.B. many of the following terms are described and illustrated in the section 'What are Mushrooms and Toadstools' (see p. 7) and in 'The Identification of Fungi' (see p. 37).

Acrid (of taste) sharp and peppery

Adnate (of gills) broadly attached to stem

Adnexed (of gills) narrowly attached to stem

Agaric mushrooms and toadstools with gills or pores

Alkaloid nitrogen-containing compound, often toxic

Anastomosing (of gills) fusing irregularly

Annulus (ring) remains of partial veil on stem

Antibiotic a chemical that kills micro-organisms

Ascomycetes fungi producing spores in an ascus

Ascospore sexual reproductive cell of an ascomycete

Ascus (plural Asci) sack-like cell containing ascospores

Basidiomycetes fungi producing spores on a basidium

Basidiospore sexual reproductive cell of a basidiomycete

Basidium (plural Basidia) usually club-shaped cell bearing basidiospores

Blanch immerse briefly in boiling water, followed by cold water

Bolete common name for toadstool with tubes instead of gills

Bracket shelf-like fruitbody which extends horizontally from the substratum which is normally woody

Bulbous (of stem base) enlarged

Campanulate (of cap) bell-shaped

Cap (or pileus) part of the fruitbody which bears the spore-bearing tissue

Concolorous the same colour as

Convex (of cap) rounded

Cortina partial veil like a spider's-web

Cuticle (of cap) skin

Decurrent (of gills) running down the stem

Deliquescent (of gills and cap) dissolving after spores mature

Distant (of gills) widely spaced

Equal (of stem) of constant thickness from top to base

Excentric (Eccentric) (of stem) off-central attachment to cap

Family group of closely related genera

Fibril small fibre or hair on cap or stem

Fibrillose covered with fibrils

Flesh inner tissue of cap and stem

Free (of gills) not attached to the stem

Fruitbody hyphal structure producing and bearing spores

Genus (plural Genera) group of closely related species

Gill (Lamella) Agaric spore-bearing tissue shaped like a knife-blade, thicker near the cap and usually radiating from the stem like a bicycle spoke

Glabrous (of cap or stem) hairless

Glutinous (of cap or stem) sticky from a glue-like layer

Habit mode of growth of fruitbody e.g. singly or tufted

Habitat local environment

Hallucinogenic mind altering, producing illusions

Hymenium spore-bearing layer

Hypha (plural Hyphae) filamentous, branching tube – the basic building block of a fungus

Infundibuliform (of cap) funnel-shaped

Lamella see gill

Lateral (of stem) attached at the side of the cap

Mealy with the smell or texture of ground meal

Mould micro-fungus species where the vegetative mycelium is visible often on the surface of foodstuff

Mushroom
a) basidiomycete fruitbody with stem and cap, the latter bearing gills on its under surface
b) common name for members of the genus *Agaricus*
c) term used to describe an edible fungus

Mycelium (plural Mycelia) vegetative part of fungus made up of mass of hyphae

Mycorrhiza mutually beneficial relationship between a fungus and a plant root

Mycotoxin poison produced by mould that contaminates food

Ochraceous (of cap or spores) ochre-coloured

Order group of closely related families

Parasite an organism (e.g. fungus) which lives at the expense of another

Pileus see cap

Polypore common name for fungi with non-fleshy (often woody) fruitbodies where the spores are produced on the surface of tubes which are not easily removed from the cap

Pore opening of tube in polypore or bolete

Primordium compact knot of hyphae which is the first visible sign of a developing fruitbody

Reflexed (of cap edge) turned upwards

Reticulate with a net-like pattern

Rhizomorph interwoven mycelial threads looking like a root or cord and sometimes attached to the stem base

Ring see annulus

Saprotrophe an organism (e.g. fungus) which gets its food from dead matter causing decay in the process

Sclerotium resting stage consisting of closely packed hyphae; can germinate to produce mycelium or fruitbody

Sessile (of the fruitbody) without a stalk

Sinuate (of the gills) notched near the point of attachment to the stem

Species group of individuals capable of interbreeding and with most characters in common

Spore reproductive cell which on germination will produce a new individual

Spore print deposit of spores found beneath fungal gills or pores especially if the fruitbody is placed on a sheet of paper or glass

Stem (or **Stipe**) part of the fruitbody which supports the cap; the base is usually attached to the substratum

Striate marked with lines or grooves; radially arranged on the cap, longitudinally on the stem

Styptic substance that arrests bleeding

Squamose (of cap or stem) covered with scales

Substratum material to which the fruitbody is attached

Sulcate (of cap or stem) deeply grooved

Superior (of ring) positioned above mid height

Toadstool

a) basidiomycete fruitbody with stem and cap, the latter bearing gills on its under-surface

b) Name for all supposedly poisonous mushrooms

Tomentose (of cap or stem) woolly

Transient (of ring) not present for very long

Truffle ascomycete fungi with subterranean fruitbodies, many of them edible

Tube spore-bearing structure like a miniature drinking straw replacing the gill in boletes and polypores

Umbonate (of the cap) with a central hump

Veil – Universal layer of tissue covering the whole immature fruitbody

Veil – Partial layer of tissue stretching from stem to cap edge and protecting the young gills or tubes

Vinaceous the colour of red wine

Viscid wet to the touch but not slimy

Volva universal veil remnants surrounding stem base

Index